C000004976

THE GREAT
AMHERST MYSTERY

**An Eyewitness Account of the Most Famous Haunting
of the Nineteenth Century**

WALTER HUBBELL

Edited
by
R.T. Van Pelt

Promethean Press

THE GREAT AMHERST MYSTERY

Promethean Press
PO Box 5572
Frisco, TX 75035
www.promethean-press.com

Copyright © 2009 by Promethean Press

All rights reserved, including the right of reproduction
in whole or in part in any form.

Manufactured in the United States of America

ISBN 978-0-9810202-4-2

*Dedicated to Gwenevere Rose, who has already discovered what
makes a good ghost story.*

TABLE OF CONTENTS

For ghosts of the dead,
Through infinite ages,
Have wandered and lurked
In earth's atmosphere;
Watchful and eager
For victims to torture.
To follow and kill,
Or make tremble with fear.

Yes, ghosts of the dead.
Revengeful and evil,
Still come in hordes
From the Stygian shore;
Entering houses
To torment our maidens;
Burning and wrecking
Our homes evermore.

But ghosts of the dead.
In years of the future,
May come from the bourne
Of the good and the great;
And tell to mankind,
All the secrets of Nature,
Psychology's laws,
And our ultimate fate.

-WALTER HUBBELL

FOREWORD

Why are we fascinated by things that go bump in the night?

Ghosts, goblins, phantoms, vampires, werewolves, the list is long and distinguished. It is almost universal, this obsession. My mother loves a good spooky movie, she is not alone, so do programmers, soldiers, air traffic controllers, and bikers. The list is almost endless.

In my last book, *Blood by Gaslight*, I presented you with lost stories of vampires - stories forgotten even by those who love tales of the undead. Here I present you with another jewel that was on the verge of slipping into the mist.

The great Amherst mystery has all the earmarks of a good ghost story. The setting, Amherst Nova Scotia, in the summer of 1878. Our main character is 18 year-old Esther Cox, the victim of a heinous sexual assault. An assault that leaves her in a state of great distress, and vulnerability. Shortly after this, things begin to happen.

The seizures, knocking, banging, and rustlings in the dark of the night. A ghost, but not your usual gothic novel spook. No, it is a *poltergeist!* The witnesses, at various times, include a medical man, clergymen, and one Walter Hubbell, a part-time paranormal investigator and well-known stage actor. Mr. Hubbell would later write this book on the haunting and publish it in 1882.

Mr. Hubbell kept notes on these most singular events, which included objects thrown from across rooms by no human agency, fires that started by themselves, and an otherworldly message, scratched on a bedroom wall, that would paralyze the stoutest heart: *"Esther Cox, you are mine to kill!"*

What would you do if your survival was determined by something from the other side, something unseen and unwanted?

What follows is an account of what occurred to Esther and her extended family. It is one of the best-known cases of a poltergeist haunting and the most famous of its time. Of particular interest is the fact that the focus of these poltergeist activities was an 18 year-old woman. Poltergeist activity is normally associated with younger people who have suffered some great emotional trauma. Yet we find the unusually older Ms. Cox is slapped, pricked, scratched, and on one occasion stabbed in the back by a folding knife!

"Why?" is the question that comes to mind. Why is young Esther Cox

the focus of such supernatural hatred? And who would do such a thing? Apparently, more than *one* dead soul.

The original ghost, the first make contact by rapping out answers to questions, claimed to be a shoemaker named "Bob Nickle". Yet before the end of the Amherst haunting, the ghosts of "Peter Cox", "Maggie Fisher", "Mary Fisher", "Jane Nickle", and "Eliza McNeal" would make themselves known to the Esther Cox and the people of Amherst.

Now, they will make themselves known to you.

So come. We are off to Amherst. Let us see what we see.

R.T. Van Pelt
Dallas, Texas
2009

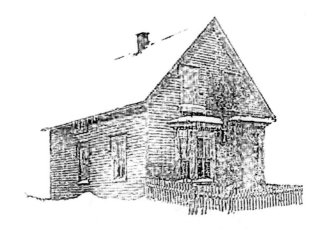

THE GREAT
AMHERST MYSTERY

Walter Hubbell,

AUTHOR'S PREFACE

The marvelous manifestations of an invisible unknown power within the atmosphere, possessing human intelligence, and performing many of the physical actions of mankind, has never been fully investigated in an impartial manner by those scientific men who reason by induction, and who have devoted their lives and scholarly attainments to the development and explanation of visible powers, such as steam, electricity and the wind, all of which lack intelligence, and only produce effects that are specific in action when properly guided by mankind.

The time has come when education is so universal, that, in our grand republic, the United States of America, nearly every man and woman is capable of reading and understanding the topics of the times. This being the fortunate state of our nation, we ought to demand of those who have devoted themselves to scientific research in other fields of knowledge some logical explanation of the hidden powers of the air - the supernatural - that has, in all lands and among all peoples, ever been the great unsolved problem of human life, and not leave to unprincipled scoundrels a field that is so full of intense interest to the human family.

The jugglers and charlatans who claim to hold intercourse with an unseen world where, they inform the skeptic and unfortunate dupe alike, that "the dead loved ones who have passed on before still live beyond the grave, and are waiting in the summer-land until we shall have joined them in the sweet by-and-bye," should be informed that science, in its true sense, has at last come to the rescue of the thousands who are being humbugged and made insane.

It has been my fate to have lived in a house where the invisible power within the atmosphere manifested its presence day after day, for weeks, in a manner eminently calculated to strike dismay and terror to the heart of the bravest man. Men and women from all parts of the country investigated, in an imperfect manner, this phenomenon in vain.

And now I call upon science, as understood and taught by those learned men of the scientific institutions of our country; to come forward and either prove my statements unworthy of belief, or that my experience had an existence outside of my imagination, and will bear further investigation. The theory has been advanced that electricity was the agent at work within the air when the wonders occurred. Some persons have claimed that "mesmerism did it all"; and still another class of thinkers have claimed for Satan the marvels that hundreds of sane persons saw and heard in the little cottage where, for weeks, I had the most extraordinary experience of my life. Some of the wonders of the phenomena I witnessed are so far beyond the realm of imagination, that I almost hesitate to give them to the world as facts, and yet that they were facts, of the most positive kind, can be proven by a complete investigation of similar cases, whenever they occur. And by then comparing the facts with the wonders I have described in this volume.

Murder, in forms too monstrous for belief, lurked within the very atmosphere; the kindling of mysterious fires struck terror to the hearts of all; the powerful shaking of the house and breaking of its walls; the fearful poundings and other weird noises, as if made by invisible sledgehammers, upon the roof, walls, and floor; the strange actions of the household furniture, which moved about from place to place in the broad light of day, and the terrible legend upon the wall, were all unquestionably the result of the action of a mysterious power, and call for investigation at the hands of men who will place their verdict on record as a truth to be believed in future ages.

Having been a professional actor since my early youth, I am perfectly familiar with all those mechanical devices which we use upon the stage, for the presentation of illusive effects so often the wonder and admiration of the public. Possessing this knowledge, gained by years of experience, and being familiar with the methods and paraphernalia used by the magicians in their exhibitions of legerdemain, I am, beyond doubt, competent to judge whether there was or was not deception of such a kind in the house where I beheld such wonders.

Truth, it has been said, is often stranger than fiction. What I have written is the truth, and not fiction, and it is *very strange*. I have not permitted my imagination to so embellish the account as to distort it, nor in any way endeavored to make it attractive at the expense of veracity. My whole account is to be read simply as a narrative of facts taken from my journal kept while I lived in the house and in which I made daily and, at many times, instant record of the manifestations of an invisible, intelligent power within the atmosphere while witnessing the phenomena it produced, and from the whole story of the mysterious affair, as told to me by the family living in the house when I went there to board; which story, in all its details, was fully corroborated by the inhabitants of Amherst and strangers from distant towns and cities, whom I saw and talked with, whose statements, in turn, were all corroborated by the facts of the case as I know them to have existed from personal experience. Nothing about the affair is supposititious, nor has anything in this work been coined for the occasion by any person and then been written up by me afterwards. And I wish it distinctly understood that I am not susceptible to the influences of mesmerism, hypnotism, or psychology in any of its forms; nor am I a Pythagorean.

Yours truly,
Walter Hubbell

AFFIDAVIT.

STATE OF NEW YORK, }
City and County of New York. } s.s.

WALTER HUBBELL, being duly sworn, deposes and says : that he is the sole author of this book " The Great Amherst Mystery, a True Narrative of the Supernatural," and that his experience as described, was an actual experience, and that deponent actually saw and heard the phenomena as stated.

WALTER HUBBELL.

Sworn to before me this
13th day of February, 1888.

A. ACKERMAN,
Notary Public No. 5,
[Seal]   New York County.

———

[Seal]

NEW YORK, March 2d, 1888.

This is to certify that Walter Hubbell is hereby authorized to print my Notary Seal on the affidavit he has sworn to before me for the purpose of attaching same to his book, entitled " The Great Amherst Mystery, a True Narrative of the Supernatural."

A. ACKERMAN,
Notary Public No. 5,
New York County,
Office, 10 East 14th Street, New York City.

CHAPTER ONE
THE HOME OF DANIEL TEED

A cozy cottage free from every strife,
Was home indeed with honest Daniel's wife.

Christmas was over. I had just closed an engagement and returned to New York to obtain another. My agent, Mr. Morris Simmonds, suggested one in Halifax, Nova Scotia, for the winter. I gave the matter some consideration, finally accepted, and became a member of the dramatic company engaged to play at the Academy of Music, in Halifax, for an indefinite period. In due time the company left New York, and after a very rough passage in the steamship *Alhambra*, Captain Mcilhenny, we arrived in Halifax, January 10, 1879. Among the members of the company were William F. Burroughs, Walter Lennox, Sr., Fenwick Armstrong, Lewis Baker, Walter Lennox, Jr., Miss Phosa McAllister, Miss Ida Van Courtland, Mrs. E. M. Post, Miss Anita Harris, Miss Ella Mayer, Miss Josie Wilmere, all well known members of the dramatic profession; also, that genial gentleman, Mr. E. B. Holmes, our stage manager, since deceased. We played in Halifax, from January 14th until March 31st, and during that short period produced 37 different plays. Just before closing our season in Halifax, I obtained three young Newfoundland dogs, and sent them home to the United States, and one of them is still in the possession of some relatives in New York. After closing our season in Halifax, where I experienced the coldest winter within my remembrance, we played in Amherst, Nova Scotia, March 25th and 26th, and in Moncton, New Brunswick, on the 27th and 28th of the same month, returning afterwards to Halifax, where we gave one performance for the benefit of our manager. Closing our season in Halifax, we went to St. John's, the well-known port of the seal hunters, on the Island of Newfoundland, arriving there April 5th. After opening our season in Total Abstinence Hall, on April 15th, we played until the first week in June, and then returned to Halifax. While in St. John's, we produced seven new plays, and repeated nearly all of those we had played in Halifax. Both engagements were under the management of Mr. William Nannery, at present, I believe, living in San Francisco, California. His brother, Mr. Patrick Nannery, was a member of our company during both engagements.

While playing in Halifax, I saw quite frequently in the daily papers accounts of a haunted house in Amherst, Nova Scotia. It was called the great Amherst Mystery, and was supposed to be inhabited by a devil. My attention had previously been attracted toward the supernatural in the following manner. In 1872, a friend lost her mother to whom she had been passionately attached; the shock of her death was very severe, and my friend, for many months, was quite prostrated from grief. Finally she determined that she would try and communicate with her dead mother through an alleged "spiritual medium." The result was that she nearly lost her reason. She went to several of the imposters, and believed all the wonders they showed her. I saw if she continued to frequent these so-called "spiritual séances," and subject her nervous system to the strain which their pretended revelations produced, she would subsequently become insane, and so I commenced the investigation of "Spiritualism," to prove to her that it was lacking in those fundamental principles which place each truth on a scientific basis. After a long series of experiments and much investigation, I succeeded in restoring her mind to its normal tone by convincing her that "modern spiritualism" was in the hands of jugglers and charlatans, who make an excellent living out of their too credulous dupes, many of whom notwithstanding, are persons of great culture and intellectual ability of the highest order.

Having been so successful in exposing a number of so-called "mediums," and my engagement with Mr. Nannery being ended, I went to Amherst to expose the great mystery and prove to the Canadians, through the press, that the devil said to be inhabiting the so-called "haunted house" had, in reality, no existence. I felt sure that in a few days, I would be able to explain the matter intelligently and end the mystery. I knew that it was impossible for anyone to deceive me after my previous experience in rescuing my friend from her impending fate as an inmate of an insane asylum, toward which, I began to think, at least half the population of Amherst was tending, so distorted were the various accounts I read in the papers and heard from persons who had been there.

Amherst, Nova Scotia, is a beautiful village situated on the famous Bay of Fundy, and is reached either from Halifax, Nova Scotia, or St. John, New Brunswick, by the remarkably well managed Inter-Colonial Railway, being about 140 miles from each city. It has a population of about 3,500 souls, and contains four churches, an Academy, a Music Hall, containing scenes, where dramatic and operatic entertainments are frequently given. It also has a large iron foundry, a large shoe factory, and probably more stores of various kinds than any village of its size in the Province. The private residences of the more wealthy inhabitants are picturesque in appearance, being surrounded by beautifully laid-out lawns, studded with ornamental shade trees of various kinds, and in summer with numerous beds of flowers of choice and sometimes very rare varieties. The residences of Parson Townsend, Mr. Robb, Dr. Nathan Tupper,

Dr. Carritte, and Mr. G. G. Bird, proprietor of the Amherst book store; also, that of Mr. Amos Purdy, the village postmaster, were sure to attract a visitor's attention, and command his admiration during my residence in the village; and although sometime has elapsed since I was last there, I doubt not but that they look just as they did then, for villages like Amherst do not grow very fast in any part of Canada; there is not the energy and push to be met with there that we have in the United States.

In this little village there was on Princess Street, near Church, a neat two-story cottage painted yellow; it had in front a small yard extending to the stable in the rear. The tidy appearance of the cottage and its pleasant situation were sure to attract a stranger's attention and always excited the admiration of the neighbors. Upon entering the house everything was found to be so tastefully arranged, was so scrupulously clean and comfortable, that a visitor felt at home immediately, being confident that everything was under the personal direction of a thrifty housewife. The first floor of the cottage consisted of four rooms. A parlor, lighted by a large bay window filled with beautiful geraniums of every imaginable color and variety, was the first room to attract attention, then the dining room, with its old-fashioned clock, its numerous homemade rugs, easy chairs, and commodious table, made a visitor feel like dining, especially if the hour was near twelve, for, at about that time of day, savory odors were sure to issue from the adjoining kitchen. The kitchen was all that a room of that kind in a village cottage should be; it was not very large, and contained an ordinary wood-stove, a large pine table, and a small washstand; it had a door opening into the side yard near the stable, and another into the woodshed, besides the one connecting it with the dining room, making three doors in all, and one window from which you could look into a narrow side yard. The fourth room on this floor was very small and was used as a sewing room; it adjoined the dining room and parlor and had a door opening into each. Besides these four rooms, there was a large pantry having a small window about four feet from the floor, the door of this pantry opening into the dining room. Such was the arrangement of the rooms of the first floor.

The doors of the dining room and parlor opened into a hallway leading from the front door. Upon entering the front door, at your right, you saw the stairway in the hall leading to the floor above, and after ascending this stairway and turning to your left you found yourself in the second story of the cottage, which consisted of an entry running at right angles with the hallway of the floor below. In about the center of this entry was a trapdoor *without a ladder*, to the loft above and opening into the entry, where the trapdoor was, were four small bedrooms, each one of which had one small window and one door, there being no door between the rooms. Two of these bedrooms faced Princess Street, and the other two toward the back of the yard overlooking the stable. Like the rest of the house, all of these bedrooms were conspicuous for their neat, cozy appearance, being all papered (except the one at the head of the stairs), and all painted, and furnished with ordinary cottage furniture. Everything about this little house would have impressed the most casual observer with the fact that its inmates were evidently happy and contented, if not rich.

Such was the humble home of honest Daniel Teed, a shoemaker, whom everybody knew and respected. He never owed a dollar to anyone if he could pay it, and never allowed his family to want for any comfort that could be provided with his hard-earned salary, as foreman of the Amherst Shoe Factory.

Daniel's family consisted of his wife, Olive, as good a woman as ever lived, Willie, aged five years, and George, aged 17 months. I think little Mrs. Teed worked harder than any woman I ever knew. Willie was a strong, healthy-looking lad, with a ruddy complexion, blue eyes and curly, brown hair. His principal amusements were throwing stones at the chickens in the yard and street, and playing with his little brother. Little golden-haired George was certainly the finest boy of his age in the village, and his merry laugh, winning ways and smart actions to attract attention, made him a favorite with all who visited the cottage.

Besides his wife and two sons, Daniel had, under his roof and protection, his wife's two sisters, Jennie and Esther Cox, who boarded with him. Jane, or Jennie as she was often called, was a most self-possessed young woman, of about 22 and quite a beauty. Her hair was light brown, and reached below her waist when allowed to fall at full length. At other times she wore it in the Grecian style; her eyes were of that rarely seen grayish blue, and her clear complexion and handsome teeth added greatly to her fine personal appearance.

To be candid, Jennie Cox was a village belle, and always had a host of admirers, not of the opposite sex alone, but among the ladies. She was a member and regular attendant of Parson Townsend's Episcopal Church, of which the Reverend Townsend had been pastor for about 45 years.

Jennie's sister, Esther, was low in stature, and rather inclined to be stout. Her hair was curly, of a dark brown color, and worn short, reaching only to her shoulders; her eyes were large and gray, with a bluish tinge, and a very earnest expression, which seemed to say: "Why do you look at me, I cannot help being unlike other people?" Her eyebrows and lashes were dark, the lashes being long and eyebrows very distinct. Her face was what would be called round, with well-shaped features. And her teeth were remarkably handsome. She had a pale complexion and small hands and feet that were well shaped. Esther was very fond of housework and proved a help to her sister, Mrs. Teed. In other respects, Esther Cox had an indescribable appearance of rugged honesty about her that certainly made that simple-hearted village maiden very attractive. She had numbers of friends of her own age, which was about 19 years, and was always in demand among the little children of the neighborhood, who were always ready to have a romp and a game of tag with their dear friend Esther.

There were two other boarders in the cottage, John Teed, Daniel's brother, and William Cox, the brother of Mrs. Teed and her sisters. William Cox was a shoemaker, and worked in the same factory as his brother-in-law. John Teed, like his brother, was an honest, hard-working man, and had been brought up a farmer, an occupation he followed when not boarding with Daniel, in Amherst.

Daniel Teed was, at this time, about 35 years of age, five feet eight in his stockings. Had light brown hair, rather thin on top of his well-shaped head, blue eyes, well-defined features, and what is called a Roman nose. His complexion was florid, and he wore a heavy moustache and bushy side-whiskers. Rheumatism, of several years standing, had given him a slight halt in his left leg. He led an exemplary Christian life, had a pew in the Wesleyan Methodist Church, of which the Reverend R. A. Temple was pastor, and belonged to a temperance society. Mrs. Olive Teed had dark hair, gray eyes, and a pale complexion, and attended church with her husband. Being older than her sisters, she was looked up to by them for advice and consolation when they were in trouble.

Life in the household of Daniel Teed was the same monotonous existence day after day. They always dined at twelve o'clock. Shortly before that hour, Esther could be generally seen seated on the parlor floor playing with little George. Willie was frequently to be found in the yard, near the stable, in the summer. Once, I remember, he was found there tormenting a poor hen, to whose leg Mrs. Teed had tied a log of wood to prevent her from setting in the cow's stall; he, however, seemed to think she had been purposely tied so that he might have the pleasure of banging her over the head with a small club, which he was doing with great persistency, when his mother came out of the kitchen, boxed his ears and sent him bawling into the house, much to the relief of the hen, who had just fallen over from exhaustion and fright.

Finally, dinner would be ready, and honest Daniel would come in hungry. Jennie could be seen coming down the street from her work; she held a position in Mr. James P. Dunlap's establishment, and went to work every morning at seven o'clock. All being there, they would sit down to a substantial meal of beefsteak and onions, plenty of hot, mashed potatoes, boiled cabbage, homemade bread, and delicious butter made from the rich cream of Daniel's red cow.

This was the happy, innocent existence led by Daniel Teed and his family. One day was so like another that the weeks slipped away without perceptible difference, and it was while they were living thus that there occurred one of the most [rightful calamities that can befall any household, Jew or gentile, rich or poor.

To have something moving about within the atmosphere, as it did in this house, is terrible to contemplate. What was it? Where did it come from and for what purpose? These were questions that not only the inhabitants of Amherst could not answer, but have been asked in vain of the scientific world. Of course there were many theories advanced, but what are theories? Often only imaginary circumstances thought out by men in an endeavor to explain mysteries when tangible facts are so elusive as to be useless.

One very remarkable fact about this house was that the power within the atmosphere increased in strength. In all other haunted houses, of which I have heard, the mystery was as powerful at the first as when it had nearly ceased, or been explained away as the work of designing persons who had a specific object in view, such as an endeavor to so injure the reputation of the house, in the minds of timid persons, that its owner would rent it for half the usual rent to get it off his hands, or a desire to frighten some very sensitive person as a joke. There were no such suspicious circumstances, however, surrounding the house of Daniel Teed. He was, in every sense of the word, a good man; paid his rent promptly, and his household was in every way highly respectable, and consequently all its members were worthy of the esteem in which they were held by all classes who knew them.

Then, it must be remembered, the house stood alone on the lot, being what is known as a detached cottage. On the front was a yard opening on Princess Street, on the right side as you entered the front gate was an open lot about 100-feet deep to the next house; on the left was a cottage 15 or 20 feet away, and on the back, the stable. I examined the cellar, and there was no subterranean passage leading anywhere. The roof -was an ordinary peaked one, and so built that both sides could be seen from the front street.

The family of Daniel Teed rarely required the services of a physician, but when any member of the household was ill, Dr. Carritte was always called. Dr. Carritte is a gentleman of culture and refinement, and of very high standing in the profession of which he is such a distinguished member and ornament. It is probable that he, more than any man, except myself, can speak comprehensively of the great Amherst mystery. He knew of and heard this phenomenon from the commencement of its diabolical demonstration, and tried all means known to the science of medicine to frustrate its demoniacal designs, and banish it from the house, in vain. His residence in Amherst was always a delightful house to visit, and he has many warm friends in the dramatic profession, in whose members he has for many years taken a personal interest and had an almost fatherly regard. He has, in more than one instance, corroborated my most extraordinary statements in regard to the doings of the unknown power, and I know will be only too happy to do so in the future, for I am fully aware that there are thousands of persons who will not believe a word I have written, and to those persons I will now say, that if they will consult the files of the *Amherst Gazette*, from August 28, 1878, to August 1, 1879; also the *Daily News*, of St. John, New Brunswick, of September 8, 1879, for which paper I wrote a short account of the phenomena; and the *New York Commercial Advertiser*, of January 17, 1888, or call upon any of the persons whose names appear in this narrative, they will find that all my statements are what I claim for them - simply, the truth, which is legally sworn to in my affidavit.

CHAPTER TWO
THE GREAT AMHERST MYSTERY

Explain all mysteries however we can,
The greatest left upon the earth is man.

Supper was just over. Mr. and Mrs. Teed were sitting in the parlor with Jennie, who presently went up stairs to the bedroom at the head of the stairs, where Esther was already in bed, having retired at seven o'clock. She asked Esther a question, and not receiving a reply, told her that she was going to see Miss Porter, and would soon return, remarking that the damp, foggy night made her feel sleepy too. As the night was a very disagreeable one, all retired to their rooms about half-past eight, and at about 15 minutes to nine Jennie, having returned from her visit, also retired to the room where Esther had been in bed for some time. Getting into bed with her sister, she noticed that she had forgotten to put out the lamp, which she immediately extinguished, and got into bed again, remarking that the room was very dark, as she bumped her head against the bedpost. She was nearly asleep, when Esther asked her if it was not the 4th of September, to which she replied in the affirmative, remarking that she wanted to go to sleep.

The room in which the girls were in bed together was in the front of the house, in the second story, at the head of the stairs, and next to the room occupied by Mr. and Mrs. Teed and their children, and had one window directly over the front door. They had lain perfectly quiet for about 10 minutes, when Esther jumped out of bed with a scream, exclaiming that there was a mouse under the bedclothes. Her scream startled her sister, who was almost asleep, and she also got out of bed and at once lighted the lamp. They then both searched the bed, but could not find the mouse.

Supposing it to be inside the mattress, Jennie remarked that they were both fools to be afraid of a little harmless mouse, "For, see," said she, "it is inside the mattress; look how the straw inside is being moved about by it. The mouse has gotten inside somehow and cannot get out because it is lost. Let us go back to bed, Esther; it cannot harm us now." So they put out the light and got into bed again. After listening for a few minutes without hearing the straw move in the mattress, the girls fell asleep.

On the following night, the girls heard something moving under their bed, and Esther exclaimed, "There is that mouse again, let us get up and kill it. I am not going to be worried by a mouse every night."

They arose, and one of them lighted the lamp. On hearing a rustling in a green pasteboard box filled with patchwork, which was under the bed, they placed the box in the middle of the room, and were amazed to see it spring up into the air about a foot and then fall to the floor and turn over on its side. The girls could not believe their own eyes, so Jennie again placed the box in the middle of the room, and both watched it intently, when the same thing was repeated. Both Jennie and Esther were now thoroughly frightened and screamed as loudly as they could for Daniel, who quickly put on some clothing and came into their room to ascertain what was the matter. They described what had occurred, but he only laughed, and after pushing the box under the bed, remarked, that they must be crazy, or perhaps had been dreaming; and after grumbling because his rest had been disturbed, he went back to bed. The next morning the girls both declared that the box had really moved upward into the air, and had then fallen to the floor and rolled over on its side, where Daniel had found it on entering their room; but as no one believed them, they concluded it was of no use to talk of the singular occurrence.

After breakfast, Jennie went to Mr. Dunlap's to work (she was a tailoress), and the rest of the household went about their daily business, as usual, leaving Mrs. Teed, Esther and the boys alone in the house. After dinner, Mrs. Teed sat in the parlor sewing, while Esther went out to walk.

The afternoon was delightfully cool, a pleasant breeze blowing from the bay. Walking is very pleasant when there is no dust, but Amherst is such a dusty village, especially when the wind blows from the bay and so scatters the dust of the unpaved streets that it is impossible to walk on any of them with comfort; that Esther finding this to be the case retraced her steps homeward, stopping at the post office and at Bird's bookstore, where she bought a bottle of ink from Miss Blanche and then returned home.

After supper, Esther took her accustomed seat on the doorstep, remaining there until the moon had risen. It was a beautiful moonlight night, almost as bright as day; and while seated there looking at the moon, she remarked to Jennie, that she would surely have good luck during the month because she had seen the new moon over her shoulder. At half-past eight o'clock in the evening Esther complained of feeling feverish, and was advised by Mrs. Teed and Jennie to go to bed, which she did. At about ten o'clock, Jennie also retired. After she had been in bed with Esther some 15 minutes, the latter jumped with a sudden bound into the center of the room, taking all the bedclothes with her, exclaiming, "My God! What is the matter with me? I'm dying!"

Jennie at once got out of bed, thinking her sister had an attack of nightmare; but, when she had lighted the lamp, was much alarmed at

Esther's appearance, as she stood in the center of the room with her short hair almost standing on end, her face blood-red and her eyes looking as if they would start from their sockets, while her hands were grasping the back of a chair so tightly that her fingernails sank into the soft wood. And, truly, she was an object to be looked on with astonishment, as she stood there in her white nightgown, trembling with fear.

Jennie called as loudly as she could for assistance; for she, too, was thoroughly frightened by this time, and did not know what to do. Mrs. Teed was the first to enter the room, having first thrown a shawl around her shoulders, for it was a very chilly night; Daniel put on his coat and trousers in a hurry, as did also William Cox and John Teed, and the three men entered the room at almost the same instant.

"Why, what in thunder ails you, Esther?" asked Daniel; while William Cox and John Teed exclaimed in the same breath-

"She's mad!"

Mrs. Teed was speechless with amazement; and they all stood looking at the girl, not knowing what to do to relieve her terrible agony. Suddenly she became pale, and seemed to be growing very weak, and in a short time became so weak that she had to be assisted to the bed.

After sitting on the edge of the bed for a moment, and gazing about the room with a vacant stare, she started to her feet with a wild yell and said that she felt as if she was about to burst into pieces.

"Great Heavens!" exclaimed Mrs. Teed, "what shall we do with her? She is crazy!"

Jennie, who generally retained her presence of mind, said in a soothing tone, "Come, Esther, get into bed again."

As she could not do so without assistance, her sisters helped her in, when she gasped in a choking voice, "I am swelling up and shall certainly burst, I know I shall."

Daniel looked at her, and remarked in a startled tone, "Why, the girl is swelling! Olive, just look at her; even her hands are swollen. Lay your hand on her; she is as hot as fire."

I have asked a number of physicians if they had ever met with similar conditions in a patient, and all replied that they had not, and added, never should.

Such, however, was the condition of this girl at the time. While the family stood looking at her wondering what to do to relieve her, for her entire body had now swollen and she was screaming with pain and grinding her teeth as if in an epileptic fit, a loud report, like one peal of thunder without that terrible after rumbling, was heard in the room. They all, except Esther, who was in bed, started instantly to their feet and stood motionless, literally paralyzed with surprise.

Mrs. Teed was the first to speak, exclaiming, "My God! The house has been struck by a thunderbolt, and I know that my boys have been killed," rushed from the room followed by her husband, William Cox and John Teed; Jennie remaining by Esther's bedside.

On finding the children both sleeping soundly, they returned to the room and stood looking at Esther in silence, wondering what had produced the terrible sound. Going to the window, Mrs. Teed raised the curtain and saw the stars shining brightly, and all were then satisfied it had not been thunder they had heard.

Just as she let the curtain down again, three terrific reports were heard in the room, apparently coming from under the bed on which Esther lay. These reports were so loud that the whole room shook, and Esther, who a moment before had been so fearfully swollen and in such great pain, immediately assumed her natural appearance and sank into a state of calm repose. As soon as they were sure that it was sleep, not death, that had taken possession of her, they all left the room, except Jennie, who went again to bed beside her sister, but could not sleep for the balance of the night, through nervous excitement.

The next day Esther remained in bed until about nine o'clock, when she arose, apparently herself again, and got her own breakfast. Her appetite on this occasion was not as good as usual. All she could eat was a small piece of bread and butter and a large, green pickle, washed down with a cup of strong black tea. She, however, helped Mrs. Teed with the housework, as usual, and after dinner took a walk past the post office and around the block and home again.

At supper that evening the usual conversation occurred about the unearthly sounds, but as not one of them could offer an explanation, they concluded it was too deep a matter for them to talk about and all agreed to keep it secret and not inform any of their friends or neighbors what had transpired. They knew that no one would believe that such strange, unknown sounds had been heard under the bed, nor that Esther had been so singularly affected from unknown causes. About four nights after the loud reports had been heard, Esther had a similar attack. It came on at ten o'clock at night, just as she was about to get into bed. This time, however, she managed to get into the bed before the attack had swelled her to any great extent.

Jennie Cox, who had already retired, advised her to remain perfectly quiet, consoling her with the hope that if she did so the attack would in all probability pass away, and she then be able to go to sleep without further inconvenience. Esther remained perfectly motionless as advised, but had only been so for about five minutes when, to the consternation of both, all the bedclothes, except the bottom sheet on which they lay, flew off and settled down in a confused heap in a far corner of the room. They could see them passing through the air by the light of the kerosene lamp which was lighted and standing on the table, and both screamed as only thoroughly scared girls can, and then Jennie fainted. And was it not enough to have frightened any woman and made her faint?

On hearing the screams, the entire family rushed into the room, after hurriedly putting on some garments. There lay all the bedclothes in the corner; Esther fearfully swollen, but entirely conscious, and Jennie lying as if she were dead. Indeed she looked like a corpse as the light of the lamp, which Daniel held in his band, fell upon her pale face.

Mrs. Teed was the first to recover her senses and, seeing that the forms of her two sisters were exposed, quickly took up the bedclothes and placed them on the girls again. She had no sooner done so than they instantly flew off to the same corner of the room, and the pillow, from under Esther's head, came flying through the air and struck John Teed in the face. This was too much for John Teed's nerves, and he immediately left the room, after remarking, "he had had enough of it," and could not be induced to return to sit on the edges of the bed with the others who, in that way, managed to keep the bedclothes in place over the girls. Jennie had by this time recovered from her fainting spell, and William Cox went down to the kitchen for a bucket of water to bathe Esther's head which was aching, when, just as he had got to the door of the room again with the bucket of water, a succession of reports were heard that seemed to come from the bed where the two girls lay. These reports were so loud that the whole room trembled from their vibrations; and Esther, who a moment before had been swollen, assumed her natural appearance, and in a few minutes fell into an apparently healthful sleep. As all seemed right again the entire family retired, but could sleep no more that night.

The next morning Jennie and Esther were both very weak, particularly Esther. She arose, however, when her sister did and lay down on the sofa in the parlor. At breakfast the members of the family all agreed that a doctor had better be sent for; so in the afternoon Daniel left the factory early and went to see Dr. Carritte, who laughed heartily when Daniel informed him what had occurred, and said he would call in the evening and remain until the following morning, if necessary; but he did not hesitate to say that what Daniel told him was all nonsense, remarking that he knew no such tomfoolery would occur while he was in the house.

As the hands of the clock pointed to 10 that evening, in walked the doctor. Wishing everybody a hearty good evening, he took a seat near Esther, who had been in bed since nine o'clock, but as yet had not been afflicted with one of her strange attacks of swelling, nor had any of the strange noises been heard. The doctor felt her pulse, looked at her tongue, and then told the family that she seemed to be suffering from nervous excitement, and had evidently received a tremendous shock of some kind. Just after he had given this opinion, and while he was still sitting by her side, the pillow on which her head was lying came out from under her head, with the exception of one corner, as if it was pulled by some invisible power, and straightening itself out, as if filled with air, remained so a moment, and then went back to its place again, under her head.

The doctor's large, blue eyes opened to their utmost capacity as he asked in a low tone, "Did you see that? It went back again."

"So it did," remarked John Teed, "but if it moves out again it will not go back, for I intend to hold on to it, even if it did bang me over the head last night."

John had no sooner spoken these words than out came the pillow from under Esther's head as before. He waited until it had just started back again, then grasped it with both hands and held it with all his strength, and he was, it must be remembered, a strong, healthy young farmer. However, all his efforts to hold it were unavailing, as it was pulled away from him by some invisible power stronger than himself, and again assumed its position under the young girl's head. Just imagine his astonishment. All the members of the family told me that they never saw anyone so completely dumbfounded as John Teed was at that moment.

"How wonderful!" exclaimed Dr. Carritte. The doctor arose from his chair; and the loud reports commenced under the bed as on the previous nights. He looked beneath the bed but failed to ascertain what had caused the sounds. He walked to the door and the sounds followed him, being now produced on the floor of the room. In about a minute after this the bedclothes flew off again; and before they had been put back on the bed to cover Esther, the distinct sound as of some person writing on the wall with a metallic instrument was heard. All looked at the wall whence the sound of writing came, when, to their great astonishment, there could be plainly read these words, *"Esther Cox, you are mine to kill!"*

Every person in the room could see the writing plainly, and yet a moment before nothing was to be seen but the plain kalsomined wall. I have seen this writing; it was deeply indented in the wall and looked to me as if it had been written with a dull instrument, probably a large iron spike. I say a dull instrument because the writing had a very uneven appearance, and the invisible power that wrote it was certainly neither an elegant nor an accomplished penman. It was similar in character to mysterious writing I saw during my residence in this genuinely haunted house, that was written on paper and then either stuck on the wall with some sticky substance by the power or came out of the air and fell at our feet.

The reader can probably imagine their utter amazement at what had just taken place. There they stood around the bed of this suffering girl, each watching the other, to see that there could be no possible mistake about what they saw and heard. They all knew these marvelous things had taken place, for each had heard and seen them with his or her own eyes and ears. Still they dare not trust their own senses; it was all so strange, so different from any previous experience they had ever had, or heard of others having had; that, they were all, without a single exception, awed into silence with fear. The terrible words written on the wall, "Esther Cox, you are mine to kill!" What could their import be? Were they true? What had written them? All that was known was that they had heard the writing, had seen the letters appear, one by one upon the wall, until the sentence was complete, but there their knowledge stopped, and everything to their understanding was as blank as the wall had been before the invisible power, that threatened to commit murder, had engraved upon that smooth white surface the terrifying sentence in characters nearly a foot in height.

As Dr. Carritte stood in the door wondering what it all meant, a large piece of plaster came flying from the wall of the room, turning a corner in its flight, and fell at his feet. The good doctor picked it up, mechanically, and placed it on a chair; he was too much astonished to speak. Just after he had placed the piece of plaster on the chair, the fearfully loud pounding sounds commenced again with redoubled power, this time shaking the entire room and all it contained, including the doctor and other persons.

All this time, Esther lay upon the bed almost frightened to death. After this state of things had continued for about two hours all became quiet, and Esther, poor girl, went to sleep. The doctor decided not to give her any medicine until the next morning, when he said he would call and give her something to quiet her nerves.

As to the sounds, and movements of the bedclothes and plaster and the mysterious writing, he could say nothing. He had heard and seen, and could not doubt his own senses; but had no theory to offer that would solve the unanswerable facts all had witnessed in the manifestations of some invisible power seeming to possess human intelligence of a very low and most demoniacal type. The next morning Dr. Carritte called, as he had promised, and was greatly surprised to see Esther up and dressed, helping Mrs. Teed to wash the breakfast dishes.

She told him she felt all right again, except that she was so nervous that any sudden sound startled her and made her jump. Having occasion to go down into the cellar, with a pan of milk, she came running up, out of breath, and stated that there was someone in the cellar who had thrown a piece of plank at her. The doctor went down to see for himself, Esther remaining in the dining room. The cellar stairs being directly under the stairway in the hall, the door to the cellar, of course, opened into the dining room. In a moment he came up again, remarking that there was not any person down there to throw a piece of plank or anything else.

"Esther, come down with me," said he.

They both went down; when, to their great surprise, several potatoes came flying at their heads; and both ran up the cellar stairs. The doctor immediately left the house, and called again in the evening with several very powerful sedatives, morphia being one, which he ad.

I ministered to Esther at about ten o'clock, as she lay in bed. She still complained of her nervousness, and said she felt as though electricity was passing all through her body. He had given her the sedative medicine, and had just stated that she would have a good night's rest, when the sounds commenced, only they were much louder and in more rapid succession than on the previous nights. Presently the sounds left the room and were heard distinctly on the roof of the house. The doctor instantly left the house and went into the street, where he heard the sounds in the open air.

On returning to the house he was more nonplussed than ever; and informed the family that when in the street it seemed as if some person was on the roof with a heavy sledgehammer, pounding away to try and break through the shingles. Being a moonlight night, he could see distinctly that there was not any person upon the roof. He remained on this occasion until midnight, when all became quiet, and he departed, promising to call the next day.

When he had gotten as far as the front gate, the heavy poundings commenced again on the roof with great violence, and continued until he had gone about 200 yards from the cottage, at which distance he could still hear them distinctly. Dr. Carritte told me this himself.

The next week it became known throughout Amherst that strange manifestations of an unknown power, that was invisible, were going on at Daniel Teed's cottage. The mysterious sounds had been heard by people in the street as they passed the house, and several accounts had been printed in the *Amherst Gazette* and copied in other papers. The pounding sounds now commenced in the morning and were to be heard all day. Poor Esther, whom the power had chosen as its victim to kill, always felt relieved when the sounds were produced.

About one month after the commencement of the wonders, Rev. Dr. Edwin Clay, the well-known Baptist clergyman, called at the house to see and hear the wonders of which he had read some accounts in the newspapers, but was desirous of seeing and hearing for himself; and he was fortunate enough to have his desire fully gratified by hearing the loudest kind of sounds, and seeing the writing on the wall. When he left the house he was fully satisfied that Esther did not in any way produce the sounds herself, and that the family had nothing whatever to do with them. He, however, agreed with Dr. Carritte in his theory that her nerves had received a shock of some kind, making her, in some mysterious manner, an electric battery. His idea being that invisible flashes of lightning left her person and that the sounds, which every person could hear so distinctly, were simply minute peals of thunder. So convinced was he that he had ascertained the cause, and that there was no deception in regard to the manifestations of the power, that he delivered lectures on the subject and drew large audiences. He always nobly defended Esther Cox and the family, when charged by unthinking people with fraud, and spoke of the affair often from the pulpit.

Reverend R. A. Temple, the well-known Wesleyan minister, pastor of the Wesleyan Church in Amherst, which the Teed family attended, also witnessed the manifestations. He saw, among other strange things, a bucket of cold water become agitated and, to all appearances, boil while standing on the kitchen table.

When the inhabitants of Amherst heard that such eminent and worthy men as Reverend Dr. Edwin Clay, Reverend Dr. R. A. Temple, and the genial and ever popular Dr. Carritte, took an interest in the haunted house of Daniel Teed, the shoemaker, it became fashionable for even the most exclusive class to call at the cottage to hear and see the wonders. They would come in parties and many heard the power make the sounds who would not allow their names to be mentioned in connection with the affair. Often while the house was filled with visitors, large crowds would stand outside unable to gain admittance because there was not room enough inside. On several of these occasions, the Amherst police force had to be called out to keep order.

Dr. Carritte, who continued to be one of the daily callers at the cottage, would have a theory one day that would seem to account for the sounds he heard and unknown power he witnessed, and the next day something would occur and upset his latest theory, so completely, that he finally gave up in despair and became simply a passive spectator. The power continued to manifest itself until December, when Esther, the victim of so much fear and torture, was taken ill with diphtheria and confined to her bed for about two weeks, during which period the power ceased to torment her and all the sounds ceased. After she recovered from this illness, she went to Sackville, New Brunswick, to visit her other married sister, Mrs. John Snowden, remaining at her house for about two weeks. The power did not follow her; and while there she was free from the torture it gave her, when moving about in her abdomen, which caused her to swell so fearfully and feel like bursting.

On returning to Daniel's cottage, the most startling and peculiar features of the power took place. One night while in bed with her sister Jennie, in another room, their room having been changed in hope the power would not follow them, she told Jennie that she could hear a voice informing her that the house was to be set on fire that night by a ghost. The voice stated it had once lived on the earth, but had been dead for some years and was now only a ghost.

The members of the household were at once called in and told what Esther had said. They all laughed and informed the girls that no such thing as that could possibly have been said, because there were no ghosts. Reverend Dr. Clay had stated that all the trouble had been caused by electricity.

"And," said Daniel, "electricity cannot set the house on fire, unless it comes from a cloud in the form of lightning."

To the amazement and consternation of all present, while they were talking and laughing about the ridiculous statement the girls had made, as having come from the voice of a ghost to Esther, all saw a lighted match fall from the ceiling to the bed, having come out of the air, which would certainly have set the bedclothing on fire, had not Jennie put it out, instantly. During the next 10 minutes, eight or 10 lighted matches fell on the bed and about the room, out of the air, but were all extinguished before anything could be set on fire by them. In the course of the night the loud sounds commenced again.

It seems that about three weeks after Dr. Carritte's first visit to the cottage, Jennie stated that she believed that the power that made the sounds and lit the matches could hear and understand all that was said and perhaps could see them. The moment she had finished the sentence, three distinct reports were heard; and, on Daniel requesting Dr. Carritte to ask the power if it could hear, three reports were heard, which shook the entire house. Dr. Carritte remarked at the time that it was very singular. Daniel then asked if the power could tell how many persons were in the room, and not receiving a reply, repeated the question in this form:

"How many persons are in the room? Give a knock on the floor for each one."

Six distinct knocks were instantly made by the power on the floor; and there were just six persons in the room at the time, they being Dr. Carritte, Daniel Teed, his wife, Esther, Jennie and William Cox: John Teed having left the room after poor Esther had buried her face in the pillow as she lay in bed, trembling with fright.

The family could now converse with the power in this way. It would knock once for a negative answer, and three times for an answer in the affirmative, giving only two knocks when in doubt about a reply.

This system of communication had been suggested by a visitor. And it was in this way that they had carried on a conversation the night the matches fell upon the bed from the ceiling.

Daniel asked if the house would really be set on fire, and the reply was "Yes." And a fire was started in about five minutes in the following manner. The invisible ghost that had spoken to Esther took a dress belonging to her that was hanging on a nail in the wall near the door and, after rolling it up and placing it under the bed before their eyes, but so quickly that they could not prevent the action, set it on fire. Fortunately, the dress was at once pulled from under the bed by Daniel and the fire extinguished before any serious damage had been done to the material. Daniel told me that when the dress was being rolled up and put under the bed, they could not see the ghost doing it.

All was then quiet for the rest of the night; no one daring to go to bed, however, for fear another fire would be kindled.

The next morning all was consternation in the cottage. Daniel and his wife were afraid that the ghost would start afire in some inaccessible place, where it could not be extinguished, in which case no one could save the cottage from burning to the ground.

All the family were now fully convinced that the mysterious power was really what it claimed to be, the ghost of some very evil man who had once lived upon the earth, and in some unknown manner managed to torture poor Esther, as only such a ghost would.

Daniel Teed explained the true nature of the torture to me, but it must be nameless here. And now to that nameless horror was added the fear of their home being destroyed by a fire kindled by this demon, with matches stolen from the match box in the kitchen and which could not be hidden from him in any part of the house where he could not find them.

About three days after the ghost had tried to set the bed on fire by lighting it with the burning dress, Mrs. Teed, while churning in the kitchen, noticed smoke issuing from the cellar door, which, as I have already explained, opened into the dining room. Esther at the time was seated in the dining room, and had been there for an hour or more previous to which she had been in the kitchen assisting her sister to wash the breakfast dishes.

They both told me, during my residence in the house, that when they first discovered the smoke on this occasion they were so terrified for the moment that neither of them could move.

Mrs. Teed was the first to recover from the shock, and seizing a bucket of drinking water, always kept standing on the kitchen table, she rushed down the cellar stairs, and in the far corner of the cellar, saw a barrel of shavings blazing up almost to the joists of the main floor of the house. In the meantime, Esther had reached the cellar and stood as if petrified with astonishment. Mrs. Teed poured what water the bucket contained (for in the excitement she had spilled more than half on her way down) into the burning shavings, and both she and Esther, being almost choked with smoke, ran up the cellar stairs and out of the house into Princess street, crying, fire! fire! as loudly as they could.

Their cries aroused the entire neighborhood. Several men rushed in, and while some smothered the now burning barrel with rugs from the dining room floor, others put it out entirely with water they obtained from a large butt into which the rain water ran, and was saved for washing purposes.

The *Amherst Gazette* published an account of the fire kindled by the power, and as the article was, of course, copied throughout Canada, as articles from that admirable paper always are, a tremendous sensation was created and genuine curiosity aroused.

Thousands of people who had set the whole affair down as a first-class fraud, began to think there might be something in it after all; for certainly no young girl could set fire to a barrel of shavings in the cellar and be at the same time in one of the rooms above, under the watchful eyes of an elder sister, out of whose sight she never dared to go for fear the ghost would murder her.

The fact that both the little boys were playing in the front yard at the time the fire was started, and consequently could not have had anything to do with setting it, was also calculated to throw an air of still greater mystery around the whole affair.

The family and Dr. Carritte alone knew that the fire had been started by the ghost. The fire marshals of Amherst were of the opinion that, in some unexplained manner, Esther had kindled the fire. The inhabitants had various theories. Dr. Nathan Tupper, who had never witnessed a single manifestation, suggested that if a strong rawhide whip were laid across Esther's bare shoulders by a powerful arm, the tricks of the girl would cease at once.

During the following week the ghost gave as much evidence of power as ever; and the excitement in the village became intense.

If Daniel Teed's cottage caught fire while the wind was blowing from the bay, when it would be most favorable for such a terrible catastrophe, nothing could possibly save the little village from being reduced to ashes. As if to pile horror upon horror, one night while Esther and the entire family were sitting in the parlor the ghost became visible to her.

When she saw him first she started to her feet and seemed about to fall dead from fright. Recovering her strength and self-possession in a moment, however, she pointed to a distant corner of the room with her trembling hand, and exclaimed in a hoarse and broken voice, "Look there! Look there! My God, it is the ghost! Don't you all see him, too? There he stands! See, his eyes are glaring; and he laughs, and says I must leave this house tonight, or he will kindle a fire in the loft under the roof and burn us all to death. Oh! What shall I do? Where shall I go? The ground is covered with snow, and yet I must not remain here, for he will do what he threatens; he always does. If I were dead-"

Then she fell to the floor, in an agony of grief and fear, weeping aloud for a moment, and then all was still. It was truly a most trying moment for the family, not one of whom could see the ghost.

Daniel lifted her from the floor, and after placing her upon the sofa, concluded that something would have to be done, and quickly too; for it was a windy night and the ghost would certainly do, what he had threatened, the house would be burned and perhaps the whole village.

"You must go, Esther," he said; "but remember, I do not turn you out; it is this devilish ghost who drives you from your home."

The family knew none of the neighbors would shelter Esther, because they all feared the unknown power, as they termed it. But it suddenly occurred to them that John White, a man who had always taken a deep interest in the terrible power as he called it, would take her into his house for the present, at least, as he had often expressed pity for the unhappy girl.

After putting on his heavy coat, Daniel went out into the snow and intense cold to Mr. White's house, which fortunately was not far. After knocking for some time, the door was opened by John White, himself. He looked at Daniel a moment in amazement, asked him in, and then said, "What's the matter, Teed? Has the house been burned down, or has the girl burst all to pieces; which?"

"Neither," replied Daniel, who then explained his mission in as few words as possible. John White said he would ask his wife, and if she was not afraid it would be all right. He asked his wife and, fortunately for the wretched girl, she did not object. Daniel hastened home, fearing the ghost would start a fire before his return. Telling Esther to put on her hat and cloak as quickly as she could and go at once to Mr. White's with him, they started out into the snow; and that was why, on that sad night, the demonized Esther changed her home.

CHAPTER THREE
FOLLOWED BY A GHOST

A maiden followed by a man's afraid;
A ghost is worse if fresh from hell he's strayed.

When John White took Esther to his home to reside, he performed a deed of charity that no one in the village except himself had the courage to attempt. Both he and his good wife showed by the kindness with which they treated the unhappy girl, that she had their sympathy. It was now January, 1879, nearly five months since the haunting of the house by the ghost had first commenced. Esther had been at White's residence two weeks, and had not heard anything of her tormentor. She was contented, and consequently happy, having improved in health very much in that short time; her nervousness and fear of the ghost having almost subsided. Mrs. White, who found her of great assistance in the house, had become much attached to the girl, and always treated her with the same kindness, and gave her the same personal attention, that she did her own children. She went to church, read her bible, sewed and did housework with the family, and was simply treated as a guest who did not like to remain idle.

Toward the end of the third week it became known as a fact that Daniel Teed's little cottage was no longer haunted by the ghost. People in Amherst all thought that as the power had succeeded in driving Esther from home, it was content to allow the other members of the Teed family to live in peace.

It was at the end of the fourth week of her residence in John White's peaceful home that, to the dismay of all in the house, and horror of the village, her old enemy, the ghost, commenced his devilish work again. One day, while scrubbing the hall at her new home, she was astonished to see her scrubbing brush disappear from her hand. When the ghost told her that he had taken it, she became thoroughly alarmed and immediately screamed at the top of her voice for Mrs. White, who, with her daughter, Mary, came running down stairs to her assistance, supposing she had fallen and injured herself. When informed by Esther that the ghost had actually followed her to their home, their feelings can be better imagined than described. Mrs. White and Mary searched the hall and examined the water in the scrub bucket, but all to no purpose; the brush could not be found.

After they had abandoned their search, to the great astonishment of all, the brush fell from the ceiling, just grazing Esther's head in its fall. Here was a new phase of the ghost's power. He, a genuine ghost, was able to take a solid substance from our material world, and render it invisible to us by carrying it into his mysterious state of existence; and now since it was known he could take one object, why could he not take another - if a brush why not the bucket? Nay, even Esther herself might be carried off by this demoniacal ghost, who was invisible to all persons except herself. But why speculate on so great a mystery here. Let science solve the problem.

For the next week, very remarkable phenomena continued to take place at Mr. White's. The ghost could now tell how much money people had in their pockets, both by knocking on the floor and wall, or on a table, or by telling Esther so that she could tell others. He would answer any question asked in those two ways, and behaved himself in a very gentle manner, until the end of the sixth week of her residence there, when he began his devilish old tricks again. He commenced kindling fires about the White homestead, and walking about the house, so that he could be heard by all persons present. Again terror reigned supreme, as in the Teed cottage. John White would not, of course, run any risk in having his new and well-built villa destroyed by fire while he was attending to business, and so persuaded Esther to remain all day long with him in his dining-saloon, which stood directly opposite Bird's book store on the main street of the village.

While she stood behind the counter in the dining-saloon, or when working in the adjoining kitchen, many new and wonderful things were witnessed by the inhabitants of Amherst, and by the strangers who had come from a distance; and many experiments were tried to prevent the ghost, who followed poor Esther every day to White's place of business and home again at night, from giving manifestations of his power.

Among other experiments, someone suggested that if Esther could stand on glass the power would cease for the time being, and perhaps for ever. Acting upon this suggestion, pieces of glass were put into her shoes; but as their presence caused her head to ache and nose to bleed, without stopping the working of the power, the idea was abandoned.

One morning the door of the large cooking-stove in the kitchen, adjoining the saloon, was opened and shut so incessantly by the ghost, that the noise annoyed Mr. White, who with an old axe-handle, so braced the stove door that it could not be moved, by any known mundane power, without first removing the axe-handle. A moment afterwards, however, the ghost, who seemed never for an instant to leave the girl's presence while she was in the saloon, lifted the door off its hinges, and removed the axe-handle from the position in which it had been placed, then, after throwing them a considerable distance into the air, let both fall to the floor with a tremendous crash. Mr. White was speechless with astonishment; but when he had recovered from his surprise he went to the saloon door and called in Mr. W. H. Rogers, Inspector of Fisheries for Nova Scotia at that time (1879), who happened to be passing in the street. After bracing the door as before, the same wonderful manifestation was repeated in the presence of Mr. Rogers, Esther and Frederick White.

On another occasion, a clasp knife belonging to little Frederick White, Mr. White's son, was taken from his hand, while he was whittling something, by the devilish ghost, who instantly stabbed Esther in the back with it, leaving the knife sticking in the wound, which was bleeding profusely. Frederick pulled the bloody knife from the wound, wiped it, closed it and put it in his pocket, which he had no sooner done than the ghost obtained possession of it again and, as quick as a flash of lightning, stuck it into the same wound. Frederick again pulled it out and, after wiping and closing it as before, put it into the cash-drawer, which he locked, and put the key in his pocket. Frederick told me this himself, and was corroborated by his father and others.

There was something still more remarkable, however, about the following fact. Some person tried the experiment of placing three or four large iron spikes on Esther's lap while she was seated in the dining-saloon. To the unutterable astonishment of Mr. White, Frederick and the other persons present, the spikes were not instantly removed, as it was expected they would be, but, instead, remained on her lap until they became too hot to be handled with comfort, when they were thrown by the ghost to the far end of the saloon, a distance of 20 feet. This fact was fully corroborated.

It was during her daily occupation in the saloon, that the ghost commenced to make the furniture move about, and that, too, in the bright light of day. On one occasion, a large box, weighing 50 pounds, was moved a distance of 15 feet without the slightest visible cause. The very loudest kind of knocking commenced again, and was heard by large crowds of people; the saloon being continually filled with visitors. I saw the box, the stove door and the axe handle.

Among other well known inhabitants of Amherst, who heard and saw the wonders at this period, I may mention William Hillson, Daniel Morrison, Robert Hutchinson (who was John White's son-in-law), and last, but not least, a most important witness, J. Albert Black, esquire, editor and proprietor of the Amherst Gazette.

Toward the latter part of March, Esther went to St. John, New Brunswick. On March 25th and 26th, Mr. Nannery's company, of which, of course, I was still a member, played in Amherst; and it was then, while Esther was in St. John, that I entered into an arrangement with Mr. John

White, to go into partnership with him and lecture on the Great Amherst Mystery, on my return from the Island of Newfoundland, provided Esther would go with us and remain seated upon the stage while I delivered the lecture. My intention being, as already stated, to expose the mystery; and make money out of it while so doing, which I considered a grand scheme for the summer season.

While in Amherst, on this occasion, I went to Daniel Teed's cottage, and was informed that the ghost had followed her to St. John. I also saw and conversed with a number of persons, who related marvelous accounts of "the power," as they called it. While in St. John, Esther was the guest of Captain James Beck and lived at his house under the immediate care and protection of his wife. Her remarkable case was investigated by numbers of persons, well known in St. John as men whose minds were devoted to occult science. Doctor Alward, Mr. Amos Fales, Mr. Alexander Christie, Mr. Ritchie and others witnessed various phases of the power and talked with the ghost by the aid of knocks on the walls and household furniture, and, wonderful to relate, claimed that other ghosts came and conversed, also, by knocking.

After remaining in St. John about three weeks, Esther returned to Amherst, and accepted an invitation to visit Mr. and Mrs. Van Amburgh, at their farm, about two and one-half miles from the village. She remained eight weeks with them, during which period the ghost allowed her to enjoy a life of the most rural repose with her kind-hearted friends in their pleasant home, which is, literally, situated in the woods. He would only knock occasionally, but never tortured her in any way. I afterwards met Mr. and Mrs. Van Amburgh at their farm, also, Mr. Van Amburgh's aged mother, who was blind, and had been so for a number of years. She must have been 75 or 80 years of age at the time, and perhaps older, and passed her time in an easy chair, where she enjoyed smoking a clay pipe, which her son filled for her. She told me she had used tobacco for about 40 years. She was possessed of remarkable conversational power for so old a lady.

Mrs. Van Amburgh was a blonde and very pleasant. I should judge that she was much younger than her husband. Mr. Van Amburgh had been a sailor, and had traveled to all parts of the world; he was about 50 years of age, tall and lean, and wore a long, tawney beard; he had brown hair and blue eyes - altogether, I found him a most agreeable man. He informed me that Van Amburgh, the celebrated lion-tamer, was his uncle; spoke of his relative's wonderful power over wild beasts, but attributed it to strong nerves and a brave, daring nature, to which was added an inborn love of all animals.

Esther seemed so happy with the Van Amburghs that all her friends hoped she would remain with them until the ghost had left her never to return. While there, she worked about the house with Mrs. Van Amburgh, played with the children, and but rarely came into the village to visit, and then always returned to the farm to sleep (the family and friends all being afraid to have her remain in their houses during the night). It was even suggested that Mr. Van Amburgh possessed an influence over the ghost similar to the alleged influence his illustrious kinsman was said to have had over wild beasts. However, I never could ascertain that such a theory had a substantial foundation. No person had any power over the ghost to my knowledge, and everything I ever saw or knew to be tried failed to check his terrible power when he chose to make a pandemonium of the haunted house.

There was one very remarkable thing about the power, however, that is worth recording here, as it may give men of science a clue. It will be remembered that it first commenced on September 4, 1878, by moving inside the mattress, on which occasion Jennie and Esther thought a mouse was in the bed, and it was always at its greatest strength as a power within the atmosphere every 28 days. The changes of the moon, perhaps, had something to do with it. I consider this mere suggestion on my part, sufficient to set, particularly, the physicians thinking.

At the expiration of the eighth week of her visit to the farm, Esther returned to Amherst, having become weary of the dull life she was compelled to lead in the woods. Believing that the ghost had left her, Mr. John White gave her a position again in his saloon, where she was kept occupied all day; and Daniel Teed took her back to his little cottage, whence she had been so cruelly driven on that memorable night, into the snow, followed by the phantom form of her old tormentor, the fire-fiend, who had written upon the wall, *"Esther Cox, you are mine to kill!"*

CHAPTER FOUR
MY STRANGE EXPERIENCE

I've heard strange tales, and thought them only lies;
But time works wonders through our ears and eyes.

After spending the winter in Halifax, where we all had the usual experience of members of the dramatic profession when playing in the provinces, we left that city of the Citadel filled with British troops, for Newfoundland, arriving at that island, after a very rough passage, April 5th, in the steamer *Newfoundland*, Captain Mylius, a Greek. When I look back now at the voyage, I think it must have been unusually rough, for I remember that all on board were seasick, except Captain Mylius and myself, and we never missed a meal. The whole company did not come with us, however; the others arriving a few days later in the *Alhambra*.

It was while playing in Newfoundland that I corresponded with Mr. John White, of Amherst, Nova Scotia, in reference to commencing a tour of the provinces with Esther Cox, having in view the prospect of taking her to Boston and New York, at a subsequent day, as the greatest wonder of the 19th century - a simple-hearted village maiden followed by a ghost from Nova Scotia.

In his letters, Mr. White informed me that Esther was again working in his saloon in the daytime, and sleeping at Mr. Daniel Teed's cottage at night. He stated that the "terrible power still produced the wonderful works of the devil," and urged me to come to Amherst at the earliest possible day, write the lecture I was to deliver, and start on our tour before the power either killed Esther or burned Amherst to the ground. I replied, that I would leave Newfoundland as soon as our season closed, which would be about the first week in June, and advised him to do whatever he could to prevent the poor girl from being murdered; suggested that he remain in her presence all day so that he could pull out any weapon with which she might be stabbed; to always have water ready to put out the fires kindled by the devil, and to advise the Teed family to take like precautions while Esther was in the cottage.

I left St. John's, Newfoundland, on the *Alhambra*, the same vessel I arrived in Halifax on. On June 2nd, I arrived in Halifax harbor, one of the most beautiful in the world, and on June 11th started for Amherst, arriving there the same day.

And it was on that never-to-be-forgotten day that I met Esther Cox for the first time. Mr. White, who had made all the necessary arrangements for us to start at once on our tour, met me at the station, and we went to his dining-saloon to dinner. After dinner he accompanied me to the cottage of Daniel Teed, where I was introduced to Mrs. Teed and Esther. Esther was very self-possessed, appeared to be in excellent health, and informed me that Bob, the ghost, said her going with us "was all right," and that Maggie, another ghost who followed her now, said the same thing.

Well, I just looked at her; that was all I could do, after such a statement on her part. I was willing to acknowledge that there might be a power of some kind about the girl, but, of course, nothing supernatural; no ghosts, or such delusions of the imagination. I let Mr. White talk about the wonders of the power, and listened to what Mrs. Teed had to say in silence. I was perfectly willing to write a lecture from what the family told me of the affair and what I could obtain from newspaper reports, and to deliver it with proper effect to as large audiences as her tremendous reputation could draw - in fact, to run the enterprise as a business transaction; but, as to believing in the ghostly part of it, that was out of the question. I would expose that; for I had been so successful in exposing alleged "mediums" in the United States, that I felt it would only be a short time before I should see exactly how she managed to humbug people so successfully as to become the wonder and talk of Canada. We finally talked about other subjects, and I left the house in about an hour with Mr. White to visit his family, accepting an invitation from Esther to call again in the evening.

Mr. White called with me in the evening, and I was introduced to Daniel Teed, Jennie Cox and Mr. Quigley, a friend of theirs. They all talked about the wonderful power, and what it could do, suggesting that we adjourn to the dining room, where there was a large table, and hear the ghosts knock.

We went, and had only been seated near the table a few minutes when an invisible power, seeming to possess intelligence, commenced to produce sounds, apparently with human hands that could not be seen. We could all hear even the scratching sounds of invisible human fingernails, and the dull sounds produced by the hands, as they rubbed the table, and struck it with invisible clenched fists, in knocking in response to questions. Esther said that Bob and Maggie, the ghosts, were both present, and requested me to ask a few questions, each of the others having had their turn. I asked the number of my watch, and it was correctly knocked, figure by figure, commencing at the left or first figure. I asked the time by the dining room clock, and it was knocked in the same manner (being 12 minutes of 10 p.m.). The power then beat correct time, while I whistled, "Yankee Doodle." I asked the date of a coin in my pocket, and it was knocked correctly, being "1876." All the knocks were upon the table and nowhere else during the evening; and we did not put our hands upon the table, nor sing "Nearer, My God, to Thee." I watched all the persons present, saw their hands and feet by the light of the coal-oil lamp in the room, and no one present knew the number of my watch, nor date of the coin in my pocket - not even myself. This was my first experience with the remarkable power known as The Great Amherst Mystery.

It being about 11 p.m., I bade everybody good night and departed, going at once to the principal hotel, where I took a room, lit my pipe, and for a long time lay awake to ponder over what I had heard. The next day, June 12th, I commenced writing my lecture in the haunted house, where I had spent such an interesting evening, and at nearly twelve o'clock, Esther Cox, Mr. White and myself left Amherst, for Moncton, New Brunswick, where I finished the lecture from what Mr. White and Esther told me of the mysterious power.

When we left Amherst, there was a large crowd at the station to see Esther off, and among the persons a man who had endeavored to get her to go away with him to give manifestations of the power throughout the country; an offer she had declined, preferring to go under Mr. White's care, because so well acquainted with his wife and daughter. This man, we believe, afterwards caused us a great deal of annoyance. In Moncton, we all stopped at the American House, and while Esther and I were in the parlor, one of the ghosts rocked a large rocking chair, while she sat about 15 feet from it. I delivered two lectures on the mystery, and left town Saturday night for Chatham, New Brunswick, Esther remaining in Moncton with Mr. White and their friends. The following notices appeared in the papers about Esther, but were not written by me, nor did I ever know positively who wrote them, never having seen them until handed to me by Mr. White, on his arrival in Chatham. It was my intention to give three lectures a week, hoping that the ghosts would knock and move objects on the stage, where Esther always sat to the "left of center," while I lectured.

THE AMHERST MYSTERY IN MONCTON
[From the *Moncton Despatch*, June 18,1879.].

Miss Esther Cox arrived here in care of friends on Friday afternoon last, and a detailed account of the manifestations and working of the mystery were given In Ruddick's Hall, on Friday evening and Saturday. Sunday evening, Miss Cox essayed to attend service at the Baptist church, but during the first singing, the ghost, which had been quiet for some days, again manifested itself by knocking, apparently, on the floor of the pew in front. When told to stop by Miss Cox, it would cease the noise for a moment, but then break out worse than ever. Throughout the prayer it continued; and when the organ began for the second singing, the noise became so distinct and disturbing that Miss Cox and party were forced to leave the church. Upon reaching the house on Wesley Street, where they were stopping, the ghost seemed to enter into Miss Cox, and she was sick and insensible until morning.

Lying upon the bed, she seemed for a time in great pain, her chest heaving as though in a rapid succession of hiccoughs, and her body and limbs being very much swollen. A medical gentleman of this town, who saw her at this time, stated that the symptoms were as those of a functional heart disease, probably caused by nervous excitement. The heart was beating at an exceedingly rapid rate, and the lungs seemed gorged with blood, so that a portion was forced into the stomach, causing the patient to vomit blood afterwards. A sound could be distinctly heard in the region of the heart, resembling the shaking of water in a muffled bottle, supposed to be caused by the blood in a cavity being shaken by the violent hiccough motion of the body. As to the cause of the affection, that is the mystery.

Toward morning Miss Cox relapsed into a state of somnolence and late in the day awoke, seeming entirely recovered. She states, however, that on Monday afternoon, while sitting near the window of a room on the ground floor, a fan dropped out of the window; she went outside to recover it, and on returning, a chair, from the opposite side of the room, was found upside down near the door, as though it had attempted to follow her out of the room. No one else witnessed this occurrence. Again, while writing, the ghost took possession of the pen, and wrote in a different hand altogether other and entirely different words from what were intended; in fact, it wrote of itself, the young lady being able to look in another direction, and not show the least interest in what the pen was writing. A gentleman, who was present at the time, asked the ghost its name, when it wrote in reply, "Maggie Fisher," and stated that she had gone to the red schoolhouse on the hill, in Upper Stewiacke, before Miss Cox did but left when she went. Miss Cox did not know this Maggie Fisher, but it seems that at one time she did attend the school indicated, and that a girl of that name, now dead, had attended previously.

Monday night, Miss Cox was again attacked and held under the power of the ghost, much the same as the night previous. A representative of the *Despatch* called on Esther Cox yesterday afternoon, but, she not being under the power, of course, no manifestations could be seen. The lady appeared quite pleasant and affable, and looked well. She considers her trouble to be a ghost, and is more perplexed with it than anyone else. She says she cannot tell, by any premonitory symptoms, when the manifestations are going to commence, is becoming rather frightened concerning it and is very easily annoyed and excited by any noise, except that which she herself may cause. If the ghost is willing, Miss Cox will leave for Chatham, by train today.

[From *The Daily Times*, Moncton, June 19,1879]

Esther Cox left Moncton, for Chatham, yesterday at noon. She has been in town since Friday last, and has been in very poor health most of the time. The Halifax *Presbyterian Witness*, we notice, speaks out strongly against Esther Cox, in traveling on exhibition, saying:

"The Amherst Mystery, we are informed on the best authority, is no mystery at all, except to persons who refrain from using their powers of observation and reason. The only mystery is that so many persons who should know better are deceived. The newspapers are greatly to blame for 'working up' this pitiable sensation. The story is now going the rounds that the girl, Esther Cox, is to be taken around on exhibition. In the name of humanity, propriety, religion and decency, we earnestly protest against a proceeding so base and disgusting. If the girl is sick, why should her infirmities be exhibited to the public? If, on the other hand, there is nothing to exhibit but very clumsy tricks of legerdemain, the exhibitors will at least appear before the public in a role not worthy of persons of character.

"We mention the case once more to protest against the wickedness of taking around a poor Nova Scotia girl as an object to be exhibited for so much money. The civil authorities ought to interfere."

[From the *Miramichi Advance*, Chatham, New Brunswick, June 16, 1879.]

Esther Cox, the "Amherst Mystery," is to appear at Masonic Hall on Friday evening. The accounts given of the singular phenomena, of which this girl is the medium, will, no doubt, attract many who have a curiosity in the direction of the marvelous.

On arriving at Chatham, I secured a pleasant place to board and arranged with the landlady, Mrs. Carroll, to also take Esther and Mr. White when they arrived, which they did in due time. While Esther, Mr. White and myself were sitting in the parlor of Mrs. Carroll's boarding house, in Chatham, the ghosts knocked on the table and promised to knock and move objects while we were on the stage in presence of an audience. It must be remembered that I only advertised to give a complete account of the manifestations that had occurred, not those that would or might occur, not knowing whether the ghosts would keep their promise or not.

On the memorable night we appeared in Chatham, I spoke, as usual, for over an hour and was delivering my peroration when an old man arose in the audience and shook his cane at me. I did not pay much attention to what he said, but caught the words, "Young man, beware." I naturally thought him a crank, finished speaking, without allowing him to interrupt me, and then, thanking the people for their attention, had Esther rise and bow her head just a trifle and then smile as the janitor rang down the curtain. I had rehearsed her in all this, and always had her carry a large fan in her hand on the stage, so that she could hide her face, in case she should commence to giggle from hysteria, knowing that persons who are not used to the stage are subject to fright, which has various forms of showing itself.

After the curtain had been rung down, I heard loud talking in the auditorium, and presently Mr. White came behind the scenes to inform me that a ruffian had attempted to strike him. I asked him if he had our share of the receipts of the lecture, he replied in the affirmative, and gave me the money, which I put in my pocket, advising him to remain where he was until I had taken Esther to our boarding house, which he did.

On reaching the street I found a howling mob waiting for us. Telling Esther to take a firm hold of my arm we started, followed by the mob, which threw stones and brick-bats at us, keeping up an angry, rumbling roar the while, as we walked to Mrs. Carroll's. I have often thought that it was simply marvelous that neither of us was struck by a single missile thrown by that mob, and wondered whether the ghosts guarded us through in safety on that eventful night. Poor Esther was entirely unnerved by the incident; and Mr. White informed us that he would go no further, that if we continued our tour we should all, eventually, be slaughtered. He was determined to return to Amherst and take Esther home to her sisters, as she was under his fatherly care. Our friends in the town - and we only had a few, three I believe, one of them being Mr. John Malloy - advised us to leave that night, while we had a chance, and we did, at midnight; going at once to Amherst.

This closed the tour of the Great Amherst Mystery, on June 20th. Esther, Mr. White and I have always believed that the whirlwind of public opinion raised against us was started by the man who wanted her to travel with him. It was he whom we suspected of having incited the article that appeared in the *Presbyterian Witness*, of Halifax, and was copied in the *Moncton Times* of June 19th, that had been read in Chatham the day of our appearance. "The civil authorities ought to interfere," it stated, but as they did not, mob-law handled our case in a summary manner.

On June 21, 1879, at seven o'clock, while the sun was shining and a cool breeze blowing from the bay, Esther and I walked into the cottage of

Daniel Teed again. She was in excellent physical health, but in a wretched state of mind, and told me afterwards that, but for my cheering influence, she would certainly have committed suicide.

Mr. White left us at the station and, finally, went into business again, but never had anything more to do with the "terrible power." I made arrangements to board with Mrs. Teed during the summer, and placing my umbrella in a corner of the dining room and my satchel on the table, sat down in one of the easy chairs, only Esther and Mrs. Teed being in the room with me.

I had been seated about five minutes when, to my great amazement, my umbrella was thrown a distance of 15 feet, passing over my head in its strange flight, and almost at the same instant a large carving knife came whizzing through the air, passing over Esther's head, who was just then coming out of the pantry with a large dish in both hands, and fell in front of her, near me, having come from behind her and out of the pantry. I naturally went to the door and looked in; no person was there; the power had burst forth again, and I immediately left the room, taking my satchel with me to the parlor, where I sat down, literally paralyzed with astonishment.

I had only been seated a moment when my satchel was thrown across the room, and, at the same instant, a large chair came rushing from the opposite side of the room, striking the one on which I was seated with such tremendous force that it was nearly knocked from under me. Just think of it; all while the sun was shining, the birds singing and the cool breeze blowing from the bay, early in the morning. I was a skeptic no longer, but was convinced that there is an invisible power within the atmosphere that men have, so far, failed to comprehend, and that at last it had struck me like a cyclone.

About this time I left the house for a short walk in the village, before breakfast. I felt that the walk would do me good. On my return, the power burst forth again, with redoubled violence. On entering the parlor, all the chairs fell over; there were seven - I counted them. I went into the dining room and all the chairs fell over. Breakfast being ready, Esther and I sat down alone, I having stood the chairs all up again. She handed me a cup of coffee, with this remark, "Oh, you will soon get used to them. I do not think they like you," with which latter expression of opinion I agreed.

While at breakfast the ghosts hammered on the table, and answered numerous questions by knocking. While there I always used the method employed by the family in conversing with them, which, as I have stated, was one knock for the negative, three for the affirmative, and two when in doubt. They were not spiritualists, however, and knew nothing whatever of that ism. While living there I tried the experiment of holding a so-called "spiritual séance"; had a number of neighbors and the family come into a semi-darkened room and join hands, while they sat in a circle and sang "Rock of Ages," and other hymns; it disgusted the ghosts; their power stopped; there were no knocks at all, and not a single object was moved or thrown.

Bear in mind that I never ceased to watch Esther Cox, and every other person in the house, to see if they ever threw articles, or made knocks in any way; and I assert, now and forever that I never detected them in the slightest deception of any kind. Her family would also watch her, not that they suspected her of trickery, but because the manifestations of the ghosts were too marvelous for the human mind to realize, and nature continued to assert her instinctive privilege. Chairs continued to fall over until dinnertime, when there was a slight cessation of manifestations.

After dinner I lay down upon the sofa in the parlor; Esther was in the room seated near the center in a rocking chair. I did not sleep, but lay with my eyes only partially closed so that I could see her. While lying there a large glass paperweight, weighing fully a pound, came whizzing through the air from a corner of the room, where I had previously noticed it on an ornamental shelf, a distance of some 12 or 15 feet from the sofa. Most fortunately for me instead of striking my head - for my head was toward that corner - as was the evident intention of the ghost who threw it, it struck the arm of the sofa about three inches from my head, and rebounding to a chair that stood within a foot of the arm of the sofa on which my head rested, spun around on the seat of the chair for fully one quarter of a minute, so terrible was the force employed to throw it and it afterwards remained on the seat of the chair. To say I was awed by this fearful demonstration of the power of the ghosts would indeed seem an inadequate expression of my feelings at that moment. I felt that I had escaped a most unnatural death, and was heartily thankful that I had been so fortunate. Truly, in this haunted house murder lurked within the atmosphere. I took the paperweight from off the chair, hastily, and requested Mrs. Teed to kindly lock it up somewhere, which she did.

All of my powers of observation were now thoroughly aroused, and I felt eager to witness more manifestations, and requested Esther to remain in the room, which she did. Reseating herself again in the rocking chair, from which she had arisen, she took little George in her lap, for he had just entered the room, and as he sat there she sang to him a well-known Wesleyan hymn. She had a sweet, low voice, and while she sat there singing and rocking, the child's copper-toed shoe was taken from his foot and thrown at me, where I sat writing at a table near the stand containing Jennie's beautiful flowers, which were always in front of the bay window.

The shoe missed me, and I put it on the little fellow's foot again and had resumed my writing, when it was again thrown at me, this time strik- ing me on the head, just above and back of my right ear; so great was the force of the blow that the spot was sore to the touch for three or four days.

The balance of the day passed quietly away. Night came and wrapped the haunted house, of which I had heard so much, in her somber mantle, and within whose walls my first day's experience was so weird that its memory can never be effaced. I awoke on the beautiful Sabbath morning of June 22nd, greatly refreshed by my night's rest, and was informed by the entire family that the ghosts never did much in manifest- ing their power on that day; for which I was not sorry, having had such an unheard-of experience on the day of my arrival that I needed rest. What with our most providential escape from the infuriated mob in Chatham, and the doubly powerful manifestations of the ghosts on Saturday, both Esther and myself were thankful for an opportunity to sit perfectly still and read, free from the annoyance of flying objects, in the air, for which we had to be always on the alert. After so much terrible excitement the calm of that peaceful Sabbath made a great impression on me. There were no ghosts in the house on that day, or if there were we did not know it. Why the ghosts did not manifest as much on Sunday as on other days, is a question I have asked in vain of all who saw their demoniacal doings dur- ing the week. Personally, I never could ascertain the reason, or assign one that was in accordance with the facts of the case.

On Monday, June the 23rd, they commenced again with great vio- lence. At breakfast the lid of the stone china sugar bowl was heard to fall on the floor. Mrs. Teed, Esther and myself searched for it in every direc- tion for fully five minutes, and had abandoned our search as useless, when all three saw it fall from the ceiling. I saw it, just before it fell, and it was at the moment suspended in the air about one foot from the ceiling. No one was within five feet of it at the time. The table knives were then thrown upon the floor, the chairs pitched over, and after breakfast the din- ing table fell over on its side, rugs upon the floor were slid about, and the whole room literally turned into a pandemonium, so filled with dust that I went into the parlor. Just as I got inside the parlor door, a large flower pot, containing a plant in full bloom, was taken from among Jennie's flowers on the stand near the window; and in a second, a tin pail with a handle was brought half filled with water from the kitchen and placed beside the plant on the floor, both in the center of the parlor, and put there by a ghost; just think of such a thing happening while the sun was shining, and only a few minutes before I had seen this same tin pail from the dining room, hanging on a nail in the kitchen, empty. And yet people say, and thou- sands believe that there are no haunted houses. What a great mistake they make in so asserting; but then they never lived in a genuine one, where there was an invisible power that had full and complete sway. By all the demons! When I read the accounts now in my journal, from which my experience is copied, I am almost speechless with wonder that I ever lived to behold such sights.

During the day a large empty inkstand and two empty bottles were thrown at me, they had been taken by the ghosts from a closet. While lying on the sofa, in the parlor in the afternoon, several needles were taken from the knitting in Esther's hands and thrown at me. A piece of cake little George was eating was snatched by a ghost, from his hand, and thrown at me three times in succession; dear little fellow, he cried bitterly about it. The ghosts then undressed him by tearing his clothes off, after unbuttoning them, at which rough treatment he cried again. I believe he could, at times, see them; for on more than one occasion I observed that he acted, as if strangers were present whom he feared. On this same day, Esther's face was slapped by the ghosts, so that the marks of fingers could be plainly seen just I exactly as if a human hand had slapped her face; these slaps could be plainly heard by all present. I heard them distinctly, time and again.

Late in the afternoon the ghosts set some old newspapers on fire upstairs: and then, as if to wind up the tortures of the day with a climax, they piled the seven chairs in the parlor on top of each other, making a pile fully six feet in height, when, pulling out one or two, near the bottom, they allowed the rest to fall to the floor with a terrific crash. The last manifestation of the day was startling; they kindled a large fire upstairs, which created some excitement. The burning papers and fire upstairs were extinguished, however, without any serious damage being done to the house or furniture.

This was my first experience with Bob, the demon, as a fire-fiend; and I say, candidly, that until I had had that experience, I never fully realized what an awful calamity it was to have an invisible monster, somewhere within the atmosphere, going from place to place about the house, gathering up old newspapers, rags, clothing, and in fact all kinds. of combustible material, and after rolling it up into a bundle and hiding it in the basket of soiled linen or in a closet, then go and steal matches out of the matchbox in the kitchen or somebody's pocket, as he did out of mine, and after kindling a fire in the bundle, tell Esther that he had started a fire, but would not tell where; or, perhaps not tell her at all, in which case, the first intimation we would have was the smell of the smoke, pouring through the house, and then the most intense excitement; everybody running with buckets of water. I say, it was the most truly awful calamity that could possibly befall any family, infidel or Christian, that could be conceived in the mind of man or ghost.

And how much more terrible did it seem in this little cottage, where all were strict members of church, prayed, sang hymns and read the Bible.

Poor Mrs. Teed! God only, could possibly have known the awful, silent agony wrung from her suffering heart. She feared for her children's lives, her household furniture, her home; and yet she loved, almost with a mother's love, her demonized and most unhappy sister, and would not, nay could not, drive her from her last refuge. Many a time have I heard Mrs. Teed say, while the scalding tears ran down her cheeks, that she believed some day all would be well again, that "God was stronger than the devil."

On Tuesday, June 24th, I was anxious to ascertain if the ghosts would cause the lid of the stone-china sugar bowl to disappear as they had the day before, and at breakfast I placed it, with the lid on, to the right of my plate. Esther and I nearly always breakfasted together. As I have stated, the Teed family, all having to go to work early, took breakfast at six o'clock. I generally arose about eight o'clock, when Esther would prepare the meal, and then, if she had not already taken hers with the others, a rare occurrence, she would breakfast with me.

When I placed the sugar bowl to the right of my plate she was sitting directly opposite me, Mrs. Teed, the only other person in the cottage, being at work in the kitchen. I removed the lid and placed it on the table beside my cup of coffee, put sugar in the coffee, and had almost put my hand on the lid to put it on the sugar bowl, to keep the flies out, when it disappeared - literally, melted into the air. I at once called Esther's attention to the fact, and informed Mrs. Teed that the lid had gone again. Both she and Esther searched the room in vain for about eight minutes, I, meanwhile, remaining at the table. Finally, Mrs. Teed returned to her work in the kitchen and Esther went toward the pantry. I watched her closely at the time, when to my great surprise, just as she had laid her hand upon the pantry door to open it, the lid came from inside the pantry, being pushed through a broken pane of glass over the pantry door, and over which brown paper had been pasted, and fell from that broken pane to the floor, a distance of fully 15 feet from the place on the table whence it had been taken from beside my plate. The pantry door had not been open while I was in the room, and yet the ghosts had carried the lid inside while the door was closed, and then pushed it through the broken pane, in the transom above the door, just as I have stated.

During my residence in the house it was an almost daily occurrence for the ghosts to bring articles from trunks and closets that we all knew were locked, and to also place articles they carried from various parts of the house into these same trunks and closets while locked, where we afterwards found them.

During breakfast the ghosts knocked upon the table and produced a perfect imitation of whatever sounds I called for, which were drumming, sawing wood, rubbing wet linen garments on a washboard; and they also knocked correct time on the bottom of the table while I whistled several popular airs. After breakfast several knives were thrown at me, but, as usual, I dodged them.

In the forenoon, while dinner was cooking, the ghosts placed a large red earthenware crock, half full of salt, that was always kept standing in the kitchen cupboard, upon the dining table. The teakettle was at the time boiling on the kitchen stove and a beefsteak frying in an iron pan, having a handle about 10 inches long. Both the boiling kettle and pan with the frying steak were taken by the invisible power, the ghosts, from the stove and placed side by side out in the yard, on a large flat stone step before the kitchen door. This occurred while Mrs. Teed was in the kitchen, Esther being near her, and while Daniel Teed was washing his hands at the small washstand kept in the kitchen for that purpose, and while I stood in the doorway leading from the dining room to the kitchen, talking to him. All saw it. The day was clear, and the time nearly twelve o'clock. The ghosts then threw two knives at me. I asked their names, and was informed by knocks that conveyed information to the effect that they were ghosts. Just after the dishes had been removed by Esther and Mrs. Teed, when dinner was over, the dining table was turned completely upside down, right before our eyes, by the ghosts, and remained in that position until I had placed it on its feet again, when the ghosts set a bundle of rags on fire in the pantry. In the afternoon, while I was in the parlor, the ghosts knocked upon the walls and floor while I carried on a symbolic conversation with them by the system already used by the family when I went there to board. And the names given by the ghosts on this occasion, as on all previous and future occasions, were the same. I put on paper each name, and whatever else they said; and the written matter upon the paper, when read afterwards, conveyed the following information: "Maggie Fisher, died aged 21 years; had been dead 12 years; said 'she was in hell,' and that 'her sister, Mary Fisher, was in the house with her yesterday,' who had been dead three years and was 19 years old when she died."

Later in the afternoon all the ghosts gave me their names by knocking, and I ascertained that the leader of them was "Bob Nickle." I am positive that a more demoniacal ghost or scheming scoundrel never haunted any house or tortured any human being as did this fire-fiend and terror of the household. He stated that he was 60 years old, and when living on the earth had been a shoemaker. He pounded under the bay window and on the floor of the room as if he had a blacksmith's hammer weighing 50 pounds to make the knocks with. I never heard anything like the sounds in my life, and in all probability never shall again.

Maggie Fisher and her sister Mary, whose names had already been given, came. The other ghosts stated that their names were Peter Teed, Jane Nickle and Eliza McNeal, and that they had all lived on the earth. Esther sat in the parlor, after this conversation with the ghosts, writing a letter to her sister, Mrs. Snowden, when she was compelled to write the following by Bob Nickle, the demon, who took absolute possession of her hand and arm and wrote in the letter to her sister, "Get out of Amherst, you bitch! God damn your *sole* to Hell!" And a moment afterward he wrote, in the same way, while still In possession of her hand and arm, "God damn Hubbell's *sole* to Hell, and yours!" All this was written by a power - the ghost - guiding her hand against her will, and was entirely different in appearance from her handwriting in the letter - which had to be destroyed - and could no more be prevented than we could prevent these demons from kindling fires, knocking or throwing things about the house. I then asked if any of them were in Heaven. They answered "No," by knocks. "Are you all in Hell?" I asked, and they replied, in the same way, "Yes."

"Have you seen the devil?"

"Yes," they replied, with the loudest kind of sledgehammer blows upon the floor.

They had cursed me and cursed poor Esther in a way about which there could I be no mistake. I was furious, and cursed I them in return, commanding them to go back to Hell and cease tormenting Esther and the family. They stopped knocking, and while I sat writing at the table threw my bottle of ink upon the floor and spilled its contents on the carpet. Afterwards all was quiet for a while; when, noticing the gray and white family cat in the room, I remarked it was singular they never harmed her. She was instantly lifted from the floor to a height of five feet into the air, and then dropped on Esther's back, whence she rolled to the floor. I never saw any cat more frightened than I this cat was at that moment; she ran out into the front yard, where she remained the balance of the day, and for several days afterwards would come to the front or kitchen door and peep in, finally venturing into the house again, but seemed always on the lookout for the ghosts. In all probability she saw them sometimes; for on several occasions I noticed that the hair on her tail and back would stand erect, when with a frightened stare into the air, she would leave the house in a hurry.

During the night the ghost, Bob Nickle, was in the bedroom of Esther and Jennie Cox while they were in bed, they stated, and pulled both of them out of bed, tore their nightgowns, stuck and scratched them with pins and knocked upon the wall and floor with those sledgehammer blows I have already mentioned. Their room being next to mine, I heard the knocking, but of course did not enter the room. Nothing could be done to prevent it, and Esther, their victim, feared to room alone. Remember, I have sworn to all I saw and heard while in this haunted house. Mrs. Teed and Esther Cox can corroborate all my statements; for one or both were always in the house with me; I was never alone; and after their daily work was done, Jennie Cox and Daniel Teed were generally with us, and very often there were visitors present whose names I have occasionally mentioned in this narrative.

On Wednesday, June 25th, the ghosts threw knives and other articles about the house and at us all. Since I had cursed them in the strongest kind of language, they were rather reserved in their actions toward us; but I supposed they would break out again, and they did. They set fire to the window curtain in the pantry and stuck pins into all parts of Esther's person. They moved the trapdoor which opened into the loft under the roof, and we, fearing the demon, Bob, would start a fire, kept water in readiness all day. Esther and I walked into the parlor in the afternoon; and just after we had gone about two feet from the door toward the flower stand, we both saw, at the same instant, a chair thrown over; and while we were looking at it, it was placed on its feet again. Esther informed me that Maggie, the ghost, talked with her during the day; but I could neither hear nor see the ghost, although I had Esther point out the exact spot on the floor where, she said, Maggie stood, and listened for the faintest whisper.

On Thursday, June 26th, Jennie and Esther told me that last night, Bob, the demon, was again in their room. They stated he had stuck them with pins and marked them from head to foot with crosses. I saw some of the crosses, which were bloody marks, scratched upon their hands, necks and arms. It was a sad sight. During the entire day I was kept busy pulling pins out of Esther; they came out of the air from all quarters, and were stuck into all the exposed portions of her person, even her head, and inside of her ears. Maggie, the ghost, took quite an interest in me, and came into my room at night, while the lamp was burning, and knocked on the headboard of my bed and on the wall near the bed, which was not next to the room occupied by the girls, but an outside wall facing the stable.

I carried on a most interesting conversation with her, asking a great many questions which were answered by knocks.

On Friday, June 27th, the knocks commenced in my room in the morning before I was up. I began to think the ghosts would follow me when I left the house. At breakfast, the same sugar bowl lid disappeared at eight o'clock, and in 15 minutes fell from under the dining room sofa. This was the third time it had disappeared and returned in as mysterious a manner.

A trumpet was heard in the house all day. The sound came from within the atmosphere - I can give no other description of its effect on our sense of hearing. It was evidently a small trumpet, judging by its tone, and was at times very close to the ears of all. I asked who was blowing it, and was told, Bob. I requested him to let it fall in the room, and he said he would do so. That night he let the trumpet fall, I picked it up, and still have it in my possession. It is composed of metal - either lead or pewter - and is about three inches long. I could never ascertain where he obtained it, nor could I find an owner for it, nor one like it in any of the Amherst stores. He must have stolen it somewhere, for he and Maggie were both continuality stealing small articles, and after keeping them for days and sometimes for weeks, would suddenly let them fall, out of the air, upon the floor. This we all saw, time after time.

On Saturday, June 28th, I wrote a letter to Mr. Lewis Baker, the actor; and while writing it, my bottle of ink was taken from the table and placed on top of the chimney of a coal-oil lamp standing on the table in front of me. I reached forward and placed the ink again upon the table, when the *letter* disappeared, and after a long search was found in the Bible, which was also on the table. Mr. Baker was at the time in Halifax, and being about to return to New York, I suggested that he pass through Amherst on his way home and witness the wonders for himself. I mailed the letter, but, unfortunately, he never received it.

One of the ghosts struck me with a screwdriver and several other articles during the day. I tried the experiment of having Esther fix her mind on an object and then *will* it to move. I chose each object myself; but it was useless. The object her mind was fixed on would remain stationary, and something else would be moved that she had not even thought of, very often being brought from another room, where I knew it had been a few minutes before, and dropped at our feet out of the air. It is hardly necessary to give a detailed account of the manifestations of the ghosts day after day, as they occurred. It would require too much reiteration and become wearisome. I am fully aware that my statements are too extraordinary to be trifled with in that way.

The *Amherst Gazette* of June 27, 1879, said: "The case has lately been watched by Mr. Walter Hubbell, who has determined to spend some time in its investigation."

One evening Dr. Carritte called, and our conversation naturally turned to Esther's case, when he informed me that on one occasion he had given her one ounce of bromide of potassium, one pint of brandy and heavy doses of morphia and laudanum on the same night, without the slightest effect on her system. This, of course, was when he tried to stop the working of the power by quieting her nerves. Afterwards, he stated, on this same evening, that all medicine was neutralized by the ghosts, he now knowing what caused the manifestations, and made her seem ill when she was not so in reality - only demonized.

One evening I sat in the parlor with Esther and Jennie, while the ghosts brought small articles into the room from all parts of the house, among them being a fresh egg from the kitchen, a shaving brush from Daniel's room, two spools of cotton from Mrs. Teed's workbasket in the sewing room, and a large number of hairpins from the girls' room. We knew that all these articles were in the rooms mentioned before being brought by the ghosts to the parlor. I tried a very interesting experiment on another occasion. While Esther and I were alone in the parlor, I requested her to place both hands in mine. She did so. "Now," I said, "Esther, look me squarely in the eyes," which she did, when I could distinctly feel a power like a current of electricity from a battery passing through my arms. After sitting thus for some 15 minutes, I asked how she felt? And she replied, "all right."

"Do you feel sleepy?" I asked.

"No!" she replied.

I was becoming so weak that I let go of her hands; and at ten o'clock, it being nearly that time when I began to feel weak; I was nearly asleep on my chair. Rousing myself, I bade her a hasty good night, retired to my room, went immediately to bed and slept for 12 hours; an unusual occurrence, seven hours being all I have ever required. I never held her hands again; once was enough. One afternoon, while Esther was out walking, she called on the Reverend R. A. Temple, and during the visit he prayed with her, advised her to pray for herself, and to sleep with a small Bible under her head. Before going out on this occasion, Esther had copied the third verse of the second chapter of Habakkuk on slips of paper, as directed by Mr. Alexander Hamilton in a letter to Mr. Teed. The special object in having her out on this occasion being to have all the ghosts out with her, while Mrs. Teed pasted the slips over all the doors and windows, which was intended to prevent the demons ever coming in again. I never knew whether the demons stayed in the house and did not go out with Esther, or whether the verse was powerless; but I do know, that one of the demons cut a triangular gash in her forehead with an old beefsteak bone from the yard that day, and that they tried twice to cut her throat with a carving knife; and in the afternoon Maggie, the ghost, tried to stab her m the neck with a pair of shears, and that she was stabbed in the head with a fork. Think of it! A young woman treated with such brutality and no one being able to rescue her. It was very hard, but we all had to bear it.

On the same night, after such brutal treatment, she went into what her sisters told me was a trance. I saw her. She lay on her back perfectly rigid and with eyes set like a dying woman; sang hymns, and said she was talking with her mother in Heaven, while the family stood weeping at her bedside. She also said she saw many persons who had formerly lived in Amherst, and gave their names correctly, the family stated; also, described the appearance of several who had died before she lived in the village, and were, of course, unknown to her. I asked her I if she saw any of my dead friends in Heaven, and she replied in the negative.

This all occurred while the Bible was under her head.

One afternoon, Mrs. Teed, Esther and myself witnessed a remarkable manifestation of the power of the ghosts to take objects from our world to theirs and afterwards return them. The instance to which I refer was so marked, that I will give the entire details. I heard Esther and Mrs. Teed talking in an undertone, while we all three were in the parlor, and asked them what was the matter. Esther then informed me, after much hesitancy and blushing, that Maggie, the ghost, had taken a pair of black and white striped stockings belonging to her, from her bureau drawer and put them on. I was astonished beyond expression at such information, and asked Esther how she knew it was the truth. She informed us that Maggie Fisher, the ghost, had raised the wrapper she wore, as far up as her knees, and that she had then seen them on her legs. Remember we were all three in the parlor, the time was two o'clock and the day was clear. I commanded Maggie, who of course, was not visible to me, to take Esther's stockings off instantly, adding that it was an infamous thing to do.

She evidently heard and understood me, poor ghost, for in about a minute, a pair of black and white striped stockings fell out of the air, and lay upon the floor before our eyes. Esther informed us that they were the same Maggie, the ghost, had had on and were hers in which latter statement she was corroborated by Mrs. Teed and Jennie. I could relate instances of similar manifestations, but think this one will suffice.

On several occasions, Bob, the demon, tormented Esther so at night that it was with difficulty she could remain in bed. I shall never forget being called up once by Daniel Teed at midnight, so that I could see for myself what I had heretofore only heard about. I dressed and went at once into Jennie and Esther's room, where the family was assembled. There, upon the bed, lay the poor, unhappy girl, fearfully swollen, and moving about the bed as if Beelzebub himself were in her. It was a fearful sight. Between her gasps for breath, she exclaimed, in agonizing sobs,

"Oh, God! I wish I were dead! I wish I were dead!"

I never imagined it could be as bad as that, and was astounded. I suggested that Daniel and I could hold her still. We tried; but the effort was useless, one demon was stronger than our combined strength. I asked Mrs. Teed and Jennie what had been done to prevent such a horrible manifestation of the power of a ghost over their sister. They replied "everything", that medicine had no more effect on her than water. We all remained with her for about three hours, when she sank from sheer physical exhaustion in to a lethargic state.

While I was there, Esther suffered several such attacks of the demon, and on one occasion, I remember, was seen by Mr. G. G. Bird, Mr. James P. Dunlap, Mr. Amos Purdy, and several ladies; and, on another, by Dr. E. D. McLean, the dentist, Mr. Fowler, and Mr. Sleep.

Once I wanted a match to light my pipe, and it occurred to me to ask the ghosts, who always seemed to have an abundance of them, to give me some. "Bob, I would like a few matches, if you please," I asked. Instantly matches fell from the air, near the ceiling. After that, I was literally showered with matches; the ghost, Maggie, gave me 45, during one day, and on another occasion, 49. I wish to state, most emphatically, that I could tell the difference in the knocks made by each ghost just as well as if they had spoken. The knocks made by Maggie were delicate and soft in sound, as, if made by a woman's hand, while those made by Bob Nickle were loud and strong, denoting great strength and evidently large hands. When he knocked with those terrible sledgehammer blows he certainly must have used a large rock or some other heavy object, for such loud knocks were not produced with bare knuckles. Of course, this is merely conjectural, but why may it not be true? We knew they carried articles of all kinds into their state of existence, and why not believe they knocked upon the floor and walls with objects from the earth, when the sounds denoted they had something very solid, and we knew they could have solid objects from our world. But I must leave theories to men whose lives have been devoted to science, and confine myself to the facts as I know them to have existed in this haunted house.

During the latter part of July the ghosts became so powerfully demonstrative that it was no longer safe to have Esther their victim, in the house. Fires were continually being started; the walls were hourly broken with household furniture; the bedclothes were pulled off in the day: the; sofas and tables were continually turned upside down; knives and forks thrown with such force that they would stick into doors; food disappeared from the table, and, worse than all, strange, unnatural voices could be heard in the air, calling us by our names, in the broad light of day. This was too much. If the ghosts continued to gain in power they would eventually drive us from the house and take possession of everything; for there were six of them and only five of us, and one ghost had proved himself stronger than two men. Daniel Teed and his wife, Jennie, Esther, and myself, not, of course, counting the two children were all who were left, William Cox and John Teed having fled before Esther went to St. John - literally, driven away by the ghosts.

One day, Mr. Bliss, the owner of the cottage, called while I was in, and informed Mrs. Teed that, unless Esther Cox left at once and took the strange power, that worked like the very old devil, with her, the family would have to move, as he would no longer run the risk of having his house set on fire and burned to the ground.

Everything that could be done to save the poor girl from the ghosts had been tried in vain - medicine, prayers, reading the Bible, and even cursing them, as I had done, proved of no more effect than so many empty words uttered by madmen at the moon. There was but one last resort. She must go. Poor, unhappy Esther heard the landlord's stern, though just, decision in silence. She had borne so much with Christian patience and unheard of fortitude, that now she was ready for almost any fate. It was her firm belief that some day the demon, Bob, would murder her; and she was possessed with the idea that the time would soon come when he would have sufficient power.

We talked the matter over; and, knowing that she was always welcome at Mr. Van Amburgh's farm, she decided to go there, and at once. So, the next morning, after packing all her worldly possessions in a large satchel, she kissed her little nephews and her dear sisters, Olive and Jennie, shook hands with Daniel and myself, and departed from the haunted house, where she had endured such torture, never to return. Poor Esther! I shall never forget her. Such resignation. She was, indeed, a martyr.

The next day after her departure, I walked over the house; examined the broken walls, and bruised and battered furniture; saw again the smoke-stained woodwork and the blistered paint; reexamined the holes burned in the articles of clothing; went again into the room where the awful power had first burst forth with such fearful violence, and there, yes, there upon the wall, I read once more that terrifying legend, "Esther Cox, you are mine to kill!" What would be the end? I could not guess.

I wondered if the ghosts were in the house. I thought a moment, and then "Bob," asked I aloud, "are you here?" I asked again, and still no answer.

"Maggie, come and knock upon the wall as you did yesterday." I listened.

Not a knock was heard.

"Give me some matches, Maggie, as you did the other day."

I waited; but not one came from out the air. I went down to the kitchen where Mrs. Teed was at work and asked her for a match. She gave me one. I thanked her, and then lit my pipe. She remarked that "the house seemed lonely without Esther."

"Yes," I replied.

"Mrs. Teed," I asked, "have you heard any knocking, today?"

"No," she answered.

I smoked; and when I looked at her again, the tears were flowing down her cheeks. We looked into each other's eyes; and then, in silence, each knew the other thought the same. The ghosts had followed her.

CHAPTER FIVE
ESTHER COX

Thy simple life of child-like homely ways,
I hope is blest by happier, brighter days.

Esther Cox was born March 28, 1860, in Upper Stewaicke, Nova Scotia. When born, she was so small that her grandmother, who raised her (her mother having died when she was three weeks old), had to wash and dress her on a pillow, and, in fact, keep her on one all the time, until she was nine months old, at which age her weight was only five pounds. When she was very young, her father, Archibald T. Cox, married again, and moved to East Machias, Maine, where he was living, in 1879, with his third wife. Esther was, at the time I knew her, mild and gentle in disposition. She could at times, however, be very self-willed, and liked to have her own way when her mind was set on anything. If asked to do something she did not feel inclined to do, she would become sulky, and often had to be humored to keep peace in the family.

She was a virtuous girl, and always bore a good reputation. Her appetite was excellent, and she seemed very partial to acids, having been known to drink vinegar by the cupful.

While living in the house I made inquiry as to whether she had ever received a severe shock of any kind; such as news of a sudden death, escape from instant destruction, or anything of a nature that would have been likely to affect her nervous system, and was told the following story, which was fully corroborated by herself.

Daniel Teed, her brother-in-law, told me that late on the afternoon of August 28, 1878, she went driving with a young man, who, for some time, had been paying her much attention; and that, when he had driven her through Amherst, and then down the road leading to the marsh, with the ostensible purpose of going into the country, he drove toward a small grove. When they had reached the grove, the young man, whose name was Bob McNeal, dropped the reins, leaped from the buggy, and, drawing a large revolver from the side-pocket of his coat, pointed it at her heart and commanded her to get out of the buggy or else he would kill her where she sat. She was very much frightened, of course, but refused to leave the buggy, telling him to get in and drive her home, and not act like a madman. Her refusal to comply with his demand enraged him so, that he aimed at her heart again, uttering terrible oaths the while, and was about to fire when the sound of wheels was heard coming in their direction. It was now growing dark and raining. When he saw the wagon approaching, he instantly returned to the buggy and drove her toward home at a break-neck speed in the now pouring rain. On reaching the cottage the girl's clothing was wet through to her body, and she was in an hysterical condition from excitement.

This young man, Bob McNeal, was a shoemaker by trade, and rather a wild fellow. I never saw him; only his picture. He was described as having black hair and eyes, and as wearing a black moustache, and, judging from his picture, was fine looking. I made inquiry as to his history, and was informed that he had a very cruel disposition, and when a boy, had been known to skin cats alive, and allow them to run about and suffer in that condition until death came to their relief.

Esther was fond of him, and always called him Bob, which, of course, was perfectly natural. When I heard that the chief ghost in the haunted house was known as Bob, I naturally thought it highly probable that the astral body of the young man, Bob McNeal, had been tormenting the girl. Those versed in psychical knowledge will understand what I mean. But, upon obtaining a complete description of Bob Nickle, the demon, who was described by Esther, who could see him, "as a very rough and brutal-looking ghost, apparently about 60 years of age, wearing a scraggy, gray beard, and dressed like any common-looking, dirty tramp," I concluded that such was not the case.

On August 1, 1879, I saw Esther at Mr. Van Amburgh's farm; she was then making a patchwork quilt, on which she stopped work every few minutes to play with the little children. She informed me that she read her Bible every day; had not seen anything of the ghosts, and was consequently contented and happy. Before departing, I advised her to pray that she might never again be tormented by the demons. She promised to take my advice, and I said, "Goodbye, Esther. Be a good girl," and have never seen her since.

On returning to Amherst in the afternoon, I met Mr. W. S. Harkins, who was managing a dramatic company, chiefly composed of the ladies and gentlemen I had been with in Halifax and Newfoundland, with the addition of Mr. Newton Beers and Mr. Joseph A. Kennedy, the latter since deceased. He offered me an engagement, which I accepted, and left that night for St. John, New Brunswick, after taking a last farewell of Mr. Teed and family, in whose haunted house I had had such a remarkable experience. We opened in St. John, during the visit of the Princess Louise and the Marquis of Lorne; and it was in the theater where we played that I had the pleasure of hearing, for the first time, the great Henry Ward Beecher, in his lecture on "The Common People." On Sunday, he preached an eloquent sermon, from our stage, to a "packed house."

I visited the Insane Asylum at Carlton, near St, John, to ascertain if any persons were confined there who were followed by ghosts. The superintendent, Mr. Andrew M'Vey, informed me that he had several who so claimed. I asked him if the ghosts ever threw objects at them or knocked on the walls, etc., and he replied that they did not, that, on the contrary, his insane patients were continually throwing objects at the ghosts. I then related my strange experience, to which he listened with great attention. When I had finished, he informed me that years before he had become superintendent, a woman, claiming to be a clairvoyant, had informed him that at some future day he would have charge of a number of diseased persons, confined in a large building having iron bars at all the windows, adding, "you see, she foretold the truth."

"Yes," I replied, "but my experience, with the supernatural, has taught me that there is a class of persons in the world whose minds are what I call 'human mirrors,' because they reflect not only the memories of others and, in that way, tell our past, but also reflect the innate ideas while still in embryo within our minds, which accounts for the fact of their being able to foretell the future, to a limited degree, simply because these embryonic ideas subsequently become the actions which shape our destiny, and then when we remember what clairvoyants have told us, we often find that what they had foretold, has indeed come true - their prophecy being but a reflection of what was to be."

He replied, that my argument seemed plausible, and that he hoped to live long enough to see science investigate the supernatural. And so do I.

After playing some time in St. John, to fair business, the company disbanded and returned to New York; I going to Boston by steamer, and thence to New York, where I was engaged by the manager of a Shakespearean company; opening in Albany, New York, as the Ghost in Hamlet, September 25th. I was so much impressed by my experience with the ghosts in the haunted house, that I could not believe a ghost on the stage should look as if he had just arisen from a moldy sepulcher, and so discarded the earth-stained drapery furnished by my costumer, and had one made that looked like a vaporous substance, to make me appear as if I was walking in a cloud while clad in armor. There was nothing to remind anyone of the dampness and decay of the tomb about the ghosts in the haunted house, and why should there be upon the stage, where we are supposed to "hold the mirror up to nature."

I traveled over 13,000 miles with this company, and subsequently, while playing King Henry VI in Richard III; and Julius Caesar, I was particular to look and act as if I was alive, and had not arisen from some rotten coffin, when impersonating their ghosts.

For months after I had left the haunted house, any sudden sound would make me start and listen; but, when I had become positive that the demons had not followed me, I became myself again. And this was the only unpleasant impression left by my strange experience. After a time I became anxious to know if the "terrible power," as Mr. White called it, had "broken out again," and so wrote to Jennie Cox, Dr. Carritte, and Mr. and Mrs. Teed. The letters I received contained startling news. Dear little golden-haired George was dead. Mrs. Teed and I had guessed the truth; the house was no longer haunted. The ghosts had followed Esther. Yes, followed her when she departed, and had been lurking within the atmosphere of Mr. Van Amburgh's old farmhouse in the woods watching for an opportunity to burst forth again.

It came at last. Esther used to visit some friends in Amherst, where there were little children, but always returned to the farm to sleep. One day, while visiting these friends, the demon, Bob Nickle, stole some clothing belonging to the children, and the articles were afterwards found secreted at the farm. Esther volunteered to return them, and had done so, and was just leaving the house for home when she went into the barn to see some person who was there. She had started for the farm when it was discovered the barn was on fire. The fire could not be extinguished, and the barn and outbuildings were burned to the ground. Bob, the demon fire-fiend, had done it. Poor girl! She was arrested as the incendiary, tried, convicted, and sentenced to four months in jail. That judge and jury did not believe in ghosts, and I was not there to explain.

Her previous good character and virtuous life, and the knowledge of so many of the inhabitants as to the true nature of her trouble - ghosts - raised a whirlwind of public sentiment in her favor and after being confined one month, she was released.

Jennie informed me, in 1882, that Esther was married and had a son, and that the ghosts had ceased to follow her. And so Mrs. Teed's prophecy had come true at last. She always said, "Some day all would be well," because she knew, "That God was stronger than the devil."

While this work was in press I heard from one of Dr. Carritte's descendants that he was dead. From another source I heard that Jennie Cox was married, and had left Amherst years ago, and that Esther has never been tormented by the ghosts since her marriage; but where she and Mr. and Mrs. Daniel Teed are living at the present time, I have not been able to ascertain. I have good reason to believe they are not in Amherst.

Esther Cox died November 8, 1912, in Brockton, Massachusetts. She was twice married, her first husband being Mr. Porter and her second Mr. Peter Shanahan. She is survived by her second husband and two sons, one by each marriage.

Editor's note:

Esther married Adam Porter on March 3, 1882 in Springhill, Nova Scotia. Together, they had a son, James Porter, who was born the same year. After the passing of her first husband, Esther remarried, this time to Peter Shanahan, an Irish immigrant, on July 23, 1896 in Cumberland, Nova Scotia. The next year Esther, Peter, and James immigrated to the United States, settling in Brockton area of Plymouth, Massachusetts, where they both worked for the city. In 1899, Esther and Peter had a son, Peter, Jr. According to US Census records, Esther worked as a laundress at the end of her life.

Most interesting to note is that in both the 1900 census and 1910 census, Esther claimed 15 as her number of children. There are no indications that she personally had more than two children, and given that Peter Shanahan was roughly a decade older than Esther, it is most likely that the other 13 children were Peter's children from a previous marriage.

CHAPTER SIX
RETROSPECTIVE

Ten years have well-nigh passed, and yet I see
The haunted house; hear ghosts in memory.

The stage should be the platform for the expression of the most ennobling sentiments, and the closing pages of my narrative should, at least, convey some sentiment of the appreciation of the many courtesies received from friends. The inhabitants of Amherst, while I was living in the haunted house, without exception, treated me with the greatest kindness and consideration, for which I still feel grateful. I do not wish my readers to think that I remained in the house all day and night watching the phenomena produced by the ghosts; on the contrary, I went out frequently to visit my numerous acquaintances.

On one occasion I remember attending a meeting of the Reform Club, where I was requested to speak on temperance. Of course, I spoke; and thanked God I was not a drunkard, but was never asked to speak again. On Sunday, I generally went to church with Jennie to hear Parson Townsend. I went only once to Reverend R. A. Temple's church with Esther, and on that occasion, Bob, the demon, who had followed her, created so much disturbance that we were compelled to leave. Every time the minister said anything about Satan or the Holy Ghost, this demon, Bob, would knock on the floor or the back of the pew, and, finally, he upset the kneeling-stool and commenced to throw the hymn books about. Esther became crimson with mortification, the congregation was greatly disturbed; the minister stopped his discourse and listened, and we left the church.

Of course, I knew nothing about those manifestations which occurred while I was out of the house, and so have made no allusion to them. Many strange things happened that I did not consider worth recording in my journal. For instance, Daniel's red cow was milked night after night in a most mysterious manner, although she was locked in her stable, and a watch kept on several occasions.

There was a band of Mic Mac Indians encamped about a mile from the cottage; and as I had once visited the camp with Mr. Fenwick Armstrong, the actor, on which occasion we had had a slight altercation with the chief, who was drunk and armed with a tomahawk, while we had only sticks to keep the Indians' dogs off, I naturally suspected one of the tribe milked the cow, rather than believe it was done by the ghosts, as some persons supposed. I did not, however, suspect an Indian because I had had hot words with the chief when endeavoring to study the manners and customs of his tribe - that would have been unjust; but, because most of them were an idle, drunken set, and did not bear good reputations.

To those who are curious on the subject, I must say that Esther could handle iron or steel with as much impunity as glass, and articles of metal were not in the least affected by contact with her, and that it was not necessary for her to be in the room where the manifestations occurred.

The night I held Esther's hands, and felt the electric current, or what I then supposed was an electric current, I was very much impressed with the discovery, so, the next day, after having had my sleep of 12 hours, I evolved a theory. I reasoned that this power which came from her, surrounded her form as an invisible vapor and permeated the entire house and all in it, even our brains, and made us imagine we saw and heard all the marvels that only really existed in her distorted mind; but when I afterwards re-examined the legend on the wall, and saw where the fires had been, and where the walls were broken, and had taken another look at the unhealed cuts and bruises on her head, arms and neck, I felt convinced that this theory was false, and that I was also mistaken about the powerful current flowing from her person through her arms into me. It was just the other way, for I was now positive that the vital magnetism from my person flowed into her and that was why I grew weak. She it was who was continually losing vital magnetism, and nature came to the assistance of her depleted power at my expense. This fact is to me established and corroborates my latest theory, which is as follows:

I believe the true solution of this great mystery to be, that Bob McNeal, who had evidently intended to commit a nameless outrage upon Esther when he endeavored to force her to get out of the buggy in the grove, was what is known among students of demonology as an obsessed person - a person whose thoughts and actions are almost entirely governed by an evil ghost existing in that part of space where all the ghosts of the dead still exist in their astral bodies, retaining there the same appearance and individuality they possessed while living on the earth. This evil ghost, Bob Nickle, could approach Bob McNeal, because his (McNeal's) system generated and threw off sufficient vital magnetism to allow a ghost to control his thoughts, and of course his actions. This being the case it is plain to me that it was Bob Nickle, the ghost, who was really acting out the one desire of his devilish nature through the organism of the young man, Bob McNeal, while in the grove on the afternoon of that fatal ride; and that, through the terrible fright and wetting she received, Esther suffered a derangement of her entire system, which caused or allowed her vital magnetism to escape, and through this escapement she became a person subject to the government of the ghosts of the dead, just as Bob McNeal was, only more so, and it was then that the evil ghost, who had been governing him in an imperfect manner, left him and gave his whole attention to the unfortunate Esther Cox, with what wonderful results this book of mine records. The fact that Bob McNeal became little more than a nonentity after Bob Nickle, the ghost, commenced to demonize Esther, is a strong point in favor of my hypothesis. Bob McNeal left Amherst, and was still living in 1879; I have already stated that he was a shoemaker. The ghost, Bob Nickle, claimed to have been a shoemaker, and would, at the request of Daniel Teed, go through all the sounds of making a shoe just as perfectly, Daniel informed me, as if an invisible shoemaker was at work in the room. I heard the sounds, but not being a judge of their naturalness simply accepted the word of honest Daniel as to that fact.

Bob Nickle, the ghost, informed me, after much questioning, that the reason he and the other ghosts did not move objects and knock while I had Esther on the stage, was, that she had stage fright, which made her lose the power through which he and the others produced all they did in our earthly state of existence.

On a subject so very vague and unsatisfactory, as the supernatural, every man who has given the subject any attention must have some opinion, and as I have had a most extraordinary experience, so far, with ghosts, and demonology in all its phases, I deem it best to give my theory of the Great Amherst Mystery now and then let others advance theirs if they care to do so.

It may interest some persons to know that Eliza McNeal, the ghost who communicated on the afternoon I talked with all six of them, said she was the sister of Bob McNeal, the shoemaker, who had threatened to shoot Esther Cox. Peter Teed, the ghost, claimed relationship with Esther. Daniel Teed had a great-uncle named Peter Teed who was burned to death in a barn many years ago. Jane Nickle, the ghost, was either the wife or sister of Bob Nickle, the demon from hell.

Maggie Fisher, the ghost, was described by Esther as a very pleasant looking young woman, apparently about 20 years of age, generally dressed in a long loose wrapper made of some material not unlike calico, of a grayish violet color. She, Esther, informed us, would frequently hang by her hands and swing from the opening of the trapdoor leading to the loft, and often leaned out of the front windows and looked up and down Princess Street. Maggie spoke Welsh as well as English. The other ghosts where described by Esther as follows: Peter Teed, a ghost with white hair and a smooth face, was short of stature and rather thin. He was very quiet and tried to prevent the others from breaking objects they threw.

Jane Nickle and Eliza McNeal were ordinary looking ghosts of uncertain ages. Their clothes were similar in appearance to women who work in the kitchens of Nova Scotia. Mary Fisher was not unlike her sister Maggie in appearance and dress. A description of Bob Nickle has been given. He was not very tall, and wore a hat.

From what I saw and heard in the haunted house, I have been led to infer that the ghosts of the dead live in a world similar to ours, and that it is to them just as material as our world is to us; that they are just as substantial to each other as we are, and that what is a solid substance to us, is to them but a liquid of vapor, and that what to them is solid is to us but air. There are, evidently, two worlds existing together in the same atmosphere, each as material and real as the other to its own inhabitants, whether ghosts or men; and these assertions of mine, I believe, will yet be proved, and be as capable of demonstration as other facts in what is recognized as positive science - provided men of science live in haunted houses, as I did. The facts can never be substantiated by investigating "Modern Spiritualism." History records well-authenticated cases of haunted houses in which no persons could live with comfort on account of the annoyance from the ghosts who haunted them. In cases of this kind, there not being any person living in them from whose system the necessary vital magnetism could escape, to permeate the atmosphere, and render the contact of the inhabitants of the two worlds possible, is it not logical to assume that among the ghosts there are those from whose bodies the same kind of vital magnetism escapes, and permeating the atmosphere of the houses they choose to haunt, makes it possible for them to come in contact with us from their part of the atmosphere, and that that is why such houses are haunted? It is my belief that some persons are born with such very sensitive organizations that they literally live in the world of ghosts and the world of men at the same time. I mean that the fact of their seeing and talking with the ghosts of the dead is not the result of an abnormal state of the system as it was with Esther Cox.

I never saw any of the ghosts in the haunted house, but heard their voices distinctly - many times, calling Esther, Olive, George and Hubbell, and heard them making the most thrilling and unnatural noises. Esther Cox could see and hear them sometimes, and then described them as being in appearance like living shadows of men and women. Little George, I believe, saw them at times, for on several occasions he would look and act as if strangers were present whom he feared. No one else saw them but he and Esther - except the cat - but all could hear them speak just as plainly as I could.

An account of my experience, while investigating what is called "Modern Spiritualism," would fill a volume. I state without fear of contradiction, that what might become a grand Psychical Philosophy, is in the hands of jugglers and charlatans. Not five percent of the persons known as "public mediums" ever saw a ghost or had a message from one. Mindreading, or thought-transference, "guesswork" and legerdemain compose "their chief stock-in-trade." These "features" of their business, aided by darkness, cabinets, music and other adjuncts, give them their so-called "favorable conditions," and in this way they have humbugged thousands and made hundreds insane. I do not deny that persons may have met "mediums" who gave them genuine pertinent communication from the ghosts of the dead; but I say most positively that no "medium" can control the invisible intelligence within the atmosphere, and that in nearly all cases, where they could not come in contact with the ghosts, they resorted to trickery, and then, when exposed in that, all that was genuine that had ever come from the unseen world through their vital magnetism was looked on with suspicion.

The greatest ill the "mediums" have to bear is to have to find out how to get rid of their "dupes," who still believe them genuine after they have been exposed. "Modern Spiritualism" was founded on manifestations of some ghosts, which occurred in a haunted house in 1848, and which were similar in character to those I witnessed while investigating the Great Amherst Mystery.

The sacred books of India, the ancient writings of the Chinese, the Talmud, the Bible and the Koran, translations of all of which I have examined, contain accounts of the return of the ghosts of the dead; and it is time science made a thorough investigation of haunted houses, and let all so-called "Spiritual Mediums" die a natural death.

The "spirit-producing" powers of the magicians, Robert Heller and Monsieur Cazeneuve - both now dead, I believe - and those of Kellar and Herrmann, not one of whom ever possessed, or claimed to possess, any "mediumistic" vital magnetism, will never be surpassed in their power to excite wonder and entertain the public by any of the "bogus public mediums" now controlling "Modern Spiritualism." What am I, do you wonder? Why, until science has demonstrated that haunted houses are but a natural form of "an electromagnetic phonograph," that give forth *power* and *sounds* that have been stored in their interior (which, of course, it never will), I shall continue to believe in ghosts.

CHAPTER SEVEN
THIRTY YEARS AFTER

During the theatrical season of 1906-07 while playing King Herod in Clarence Bennett's masterpiece, "Jerusalem, the Holy City," the grandest historical tragedy ever written from a Biblical source, I was frequently questioned by persons in California, in fact in all the states beyond the Rocky Mountains and particularly eastward of them, concerning my book *The Great Amherst Mystery*. Wherever I appear there is always some person desirous of obtaining more information more facts about Esther Cox, the girl who was followed by ghosts of the dead in Nova Scotia, and whom they tortured, stabbed and even tried to kill.

During the season of 1907-08, I played Aguila, the Indian in Clarence Bennett's Romantic Mexican play "A Royal Slave." On May 16, 1908, I appeared as the Indian in the "Royal Slave" at the Academy of Music in Amherst, it being my first visit to the town since I lived in the haunted home of Esther Cox, known to the world as the Great Amherst Mystery, 29 years ago.

After closing the season in Yarmouth, my supporting company returned to the United States, and I went to Digby, Nova Scotia, where I "boarded" the Steamer *Prince Rupert* for St. John, New Brunswick, and there took a train on the Intercolonial Railway for Amherst, 137 miles distant, arriving the same day, June 2nd. On arriving in Amherst I went at once to the little brown cottage on Princess Street, between Church and Havelock, Number 6, high peeked roof, low paling fence, vine growing around the front door, big bay window. Can I ever forget it? No! Never! Never! for in this little cottage where I now am at this exact moment of time, 11.30 a. m., I had the most remarkable experience of my life years ago. Yes, this is Monday, June 22, 1908, and I am sitting at a small table near the window writing these very words with an indelible pencil in great haste, so that I may give my Canadian publisher, Mr. J. H. Froggatt, proprietor and manager of *The Amherst Daily News*, the additions to my book as agreed upon before leaving here for New York City, which I shall do tomorrow, going first to Boston, Massachusetts, the "Athens of America." As I sit here by the window writing these closing lines, I recall the fact that it was in this very room 29 years ago that I so often saw Esther Cox dreadfully tortured by Bob, the demon ghost, who confessed that he and his comrade ghosts had come from Hell to play.

It was in this very room that Bob, the demon, gave me the small trumpet he had been blowing all day. Here, too, he and Maggie Fisher, the ghost, marked Jane and Esther Cox from "head to foot" with "signs of the Cross" in bloody scratches with a pin or hair pin, and it was here that everything as described in this book, as occurring in Esther Cox's bedroom took place, for this was her bedroom, during the six weeks I lived in this house in 1879. Her bedroom! I might have written: "It was her torture chamber."

Mrs. Olive Teed has written me a letter. It was written yesterday, June 21st, and is now in the printer's hands; for they are now setting the type to make the plates to print from, and in her letter she gives an account of what the ghosts did to her sister Esther Cox, one moonlight Sunday night, after I had left Amherst for St. John, New Brunswick, which I did on August 1, 1879.

I have now been living in Amherst for three weeks, and during that time have slept in this same room of dreadful recollections. If the walls of rooms could only tell of or show again the awful scenes and deeds enacted in them, the sufferings of Esther Cox, in this my present bedroom, would probably give me the nightmare or some other kind of phantasmagoria or hallucination every night, but I am sure they cannot "speak" in any way or form but are as silent as the eternal silence of a tomb, because I sleep well. It has interested me to ascertain the past history of this cottage. It was built by Louis Fillmore, 35 or 40 years ago, and has had several owners and tenants, among whom I may mention McClellan, John Pipes and Daniel Teed as tenants, and I. Z. Bliss, who owned and rented it to Daniel Teed, and finally came here to live after Teed had moved away, and then died here himself about 15 years ago, leaving Robert W. Davis, his stepson who lived with him in the house, in possession. The next tenant, Mrs. Rebecca Cahill, has lived here about 10 years. Her household consists of her son Mr. John Cahill, his wife Mrs. Myrtle Cahill, their dear little daughter Audrey, one year old, and a grown up daughter, Miss Sadie May Betts, and it is due entirely to their kindness that I am allowed to rent this room, as a favor, that is fully appreciated by me, and the more so perhaps because they do not rent rooms or take boarders. I came to them a stranger and they took me in. Mr. Cahill's room is the one at the head of the stairway as you come up to the left. It is the room in which the ghosts first demonstrated their awe-inspiring power and it was upon the walls of that room that Bob Nickle, the demon ghost, fire-fiend and tormentor of the household, wrote with the iron spike that terrifying legend, "Esther Cox, you are mine to kill," about 30 years ago. He wrote it upon the bare plaster of the wall, as I have already stated in this book. Hundreds of persons read it as I did many times. On examining the walls on which it had been written I found to my great disappointment it had been covered over with paper. At my suggestion Mr.

Cahill had the wall paper removed from the wall, which we then examined, and found that the room had been re-papered four or five times and that the wall itself had been given a heavy coating of white paint, apparently to cover, hide and obliterate the legend that probably had become obnoxious to some former tenant or to Bliss himself long before he died. If the legend had been found, a photographic reproduction would be now before you who read these lines. As to the story of this cottage I would further state that no murder was ever committed in it, nor have disreputable persons ever lived in it. It cost about $1,000 to build and the lot is probably worth a considerable sum. The present owner is Charles Tupper Hillson.

On returning to Amherst after my long absence I found what I had left a village of about 3,500 to be now a town of nearly 10,000 inhabitants, with all the modern improvements of civilization; many new and costly churches, stores and private dwellings and several industrial plants of immense magnitude and value aggregating millions of dollars.

Daniel Teed and his devoted wife Olive, I found well, prosperous and happy, and he no longer lame as when I knew him first, but able to walk as well and as fast as his son William Teed, now of course a young man, and a fine one too, fond of trotting horses and of life. Four fine daughters have come into the Teed family and two of them have grown to womanhood, all since I was last here.

Jane Cox left Amherst years ago and married in the United States, where she lives.

Esther Cox married in Springhill, Nova Scotia, many years ago. Her husband died and she married again and lives with her second husband and children in the United States.

After Bob, the demon-ghost, was finally scared away from Esther by the incantations and conjurations of an "Indian Medicine Man" or "Witch Doctor" and promised never to follow or molest her again, for it is true that as "death" does not change a man's nature or personality, a superstitious man must necessarily become a superstitious ghost, he, this same Bob, the very worst and most malicious ghost I ever met with, knew, or heard of, went back again to his old friend, the young man whom he obsessed for many years before Esther Cox became his most unwilling victim.

During the year from 1878 to 1879 the young man led a quiet uneventful life because his "guiding demon" "was working" in the vital magnetic aura of Esther Cox, but after this demon Bob finally left her forever, he returned to his "old victim" in whose presence and through whose personality he is now, in the year 1908, the "invisible terror" of the neighborhood in which he lives. My explanation of this great Amherst Mystery as given in the first edition of my book, first published in 1888 has stood the test of time and is just as true and correct now in 1908 - after

20 years - as it was then. This is all well known and perfectly clear now to many brave strong-minded men in Amherst, Sackville, New Brunswick, and elsewhere in Canada and the United States, who are willing to "back" and prove my verdict as correct and true - and they will do so in the future, now more than ever because they stand for truth.

My three weeks vacation now ended has been delightfully spent in Amherst where I met many old friends and found numerous new ones. Among the former I may mention Mr. Golding Bird and Mrs. Golding Bird, also Major J. Albert Black and Mrs. Black, Mr. Daniel Teed and Mrs. Olive Teed, and each and all of the gentlemen whose names are signed to the "Document" delivered to me by the Citizens of Amherst for publication.

Editor's Note:

After the events of Amherst, Walter Hubbell continued his career as an actor, eventually settling in the New York area. Hubbell's interest in spiritualism remained strong throughout his lifetime, and he would go on to participate in other parapsychological investigations. To date, his celebrated book on the Amherst haunting has been published and reprinted in at least 12 editions, including the one you hold in your hands.

Walter Hubbell died on January 25, 1932, in the Freeport area of Long Island, New York, at the age of 80.

APPENDIX I
ADDITIONAL COMMENTARY

THE SUPERMUNDANE
BY WALTER HUBBELL

[From *The Esoteric Magazine*, Vol. III., page 74. Boston, 1889.]

There is at present so much interest displayed in the pursuit of the supernatural, and this in all probability will, in the near future, be so materially augmented, that it is desirable to get as much material as possible before the public, in order that it may be able to satisfy the demand, which each man will shortly make to know, beyond peradventure, whether or not his ego, clothed in a personality peculiar to itself, shall survive death. The great mass of matter to be used in this final adjudication must, of very necessity, like so many other things, be taken upon testimony; and, in many instances, there will be little save consistency and internal coherence, or the lack thereof, to attest the truth or falsity of the records rendered. There is no better way, however, than to peruse everything, tendered as testimony, in an impartial, though critical manner lending most significance and credence to those phenomena which are found most frequently recorded. The speculating eye of the nineteenth century has ceased to blink those solemn Oriental asseverations that occultism is a verity, and is gradually opening to a realization of the fact that even the Occident has more things than are dreamt of in its philosophy. As yet, to be sure, much of the subject must of necessity be hypothetical, and many pseudo-explanatory ideas addressed to the solution of what is now pretty generally known to exist will be promulgated. Many of these will be fallacious, some one may be right, and all will confer the benefit of attracting attention to a subject co-important with our very existence. "The Supermundane" is published in the hope that it may be found useful in one of these lines. -Ed.

The marvelous manifestation of an invisible power within the atmosphere possessing human intelligence, and performing many of the physical actions of mankind in haunted houses has never been investigated in an impartial manner by those scientific men who reason by induction, and devote their lives and scholarly attainments to the development and explanation of visible powers, such, for instance, as hydraulics, steam and electricity, none of which ever produce effects that are specific in action unless properly guided by mankind. In this age of scientific achievement, the time is certainly at hand when all the nations of the earth should come to some definitely unanimous conclusion upon the supermundane, and I propose in this article to give a logical explanation of the "powers of the air," so that the alleged supernatural, that has in all lands ever been the great unsolvable problem of human life, may be understood by all.

It seems to me that it is almost criminal negligence on my part to leave to the jugglers and charlatans who claim to hold intercourse with the inhabitants of an unseen world a field that is so full of intense interest to the entire human family, without at least offering my logical hypothesis to the world. It has been my good fortune to have lived in a house where an invisible, intelligent power within the atmosphere manifested its presence day after day for weeks, in a manner eminently calculated to strike terror and dismay into the hearts of the bravest men.

The theory has been advanced that electricity was the agent at work within the air when the wonders occurred. Some persons claimed that it was all the result of hypnotism, or some other form of psychology, while others declared that it must have been Satan himself who produced the marvels that hundreds of persons saw and heard, in the little cottage in Amherst, Nova Scotia, where, for weeks, I had the most remarkable - the most extraordinary experience of my life.

Some of the wonders witnessed were so far beyond the realm of imagination that I almost hesitated to give them to the world as facts, and yet that they were facts of the most incontrovertible kind, has been proved by reliable witnesses. All my assertions can be fully substantiated by a complete investigation of similar cases by scientists, whenever such cases occur, and, as my experience is by no means an isolated one, it is but reasonable to assume that in the future there will be as many - if not more - haunted houses than in the past.

Having been a professional actor since my early youth, I am perfectly familiar with all the mechanical devices we use upon the stage to produce the illusive effects that are so often the wonder and admiration of the public. Possessing this knowledge gained by years of experience, and being perfectly familiar with the methods and paraphernalia used by magicians in their exhibitions of legerdemain, I am, beyond doubt, competent to judge whether there was, or was not, deception of such a kind in the house where I beheld wonders almost too stupendous for belief, and I assert most positively that no deception of any kind was practiced.

It is not my intention to give in this article a detailed account of the many haunted houses with which I am familiar, but rather to confine myself to the one in which I lived, and in which I had such a strange and startling experience. It is to my explanation of the cause of this particular haunted house that I shall direct the reader's attention. However, before giving my explanation of haunted houses in general, it will be necessary to state that, in the house where my terrible experience occurred, horrors in forms too monstrous for belief lurked within the atmosphere; the kindling of mysterious fires struck terror to the hearts of all; the trembling and shaking of the house, and the breaking of its walls; the fearful poundings and other weird noises, as if made by invisible sledgehammers upon the roof, walls and floor; the strange actions of the household furniture, which moved about in the broad light of day; the shrill and awful voices in the air; and a terrifying legend written upon the wall, were all unquestionably the result of the action of a mysterious, intelligent power existing within the atmosphere, and I claim that the power producing these weird results was, in the instance that came under my personal observation, nothing more nor less than ghosts of the dead; and I also believe that houses in the past have been haunted by ghosts of the dead, and that, at a subsequent day when houses so infested shall have been properly investigated by scientists using my hypothesis as the basis of their explanation, their verdict will attest my theory, as to the cause and explanation of haunted houses, a truth to be believed in future ages, solving for all time the great problem, is there another world and a life hereafter?

In these days of agnostics and iconoclasts, all infidels and atheists who have read thus far will doubtless consider all that I have written as but the senseless wanderings of a weird or irreverent imagination, which has conjured up the alleged superstitions of the dark ages. But, to those readers who believe in the divine origin of the Bible, my explanation will perhaps be of interest, and I hope of value.

As hundreds of thousands of persons, otherwise of the very highest attainments in science, literature and art, do not know that they possess astral bodies, I must explain, as part of my hypothesis, that the astral body of a human being is born of, or derived from, the astral bodies of his or her parents, just as truly as his or her physical body is born of, or derived from, their physical bodies. I claim that this fact is established by the many recorded cases of "marking," in which the influence of the mother's emotions so affects her unborn offspring as to forever stamp it with distinct traits of character, and, in some instances, with peculiar physical appearance. Now, as there is no neutral connection between the mother and fetus, how can it be possible that a mother, or in fact either parent, should in any way transmit mental characteristics, unless the offspring is born of its parents' astral as well as their physical bodies. Any other hypothesis must seem preposterous, when accounting for mental characteristics; for it is a well-known fact in heredity that many persons resemble their mother physically, and yet possess their father's mental structure, and *vice versa*, without possessing any of those abnormal physical marks known to come from emotional, prenatal influences.

Furthermore, I claim that it is the astral body of a human being that becomes a ghost in the other world, after it has been released from this by death, and that, during our life on earth, it is this astral body that gives form to the physical body, and to each of its members, head, face, hands, arms, legs, feet, and so on; hence it follows that the ghosts of the dead are identical in appearance with the physical forms which they cast off at death.

As to the existence of the astral body, it is a fact that any person can ascertain for himself by asking a man who has lost a limb, or a portion of one, if he ever feels the actual presence of the severed member. He will answer, "Yes, I do sometimes," and the reason he feels its presence is obvious. The astral - or ghostly limb - or portion of it, is still there, and under certain vitomagnetic conditions hereafter fully explained - its actual presence is manifest. From what knowledge I have acquired on the subject, and what I have seen and heard in haunted houses, I am fully convinced that there is another world, and a life hereafter, and that it is the men, women and children who die in this world that actually live in the other world - the world of ghosts.

Also, that to these ghosts their world is just as material as our world is to us; that they are just as substantial beings to each other as ghosts, as we are to each other as men; and that what is a solid substance to us as men, is to the ghosts but a liquid or vapor; while what to them is solid substance is to us but air.

Or, to put it more comprehensively, perhaps: the two existing together in the atmosphere, are each as material and real as the other to the inhabitants of their own environment, whether they be ghosts or men.

The modern medical theory, that all persons who claim to see or hear ghosts of the dead are deranged, is not tenable. Nor does it prove that there are no ghosts, because we know that deranged persons often claim to see and hear them, for there is no reason why an insane person should not see and hear a ghost just the same as a sane person does.

This statement may at first seem paradoxical, but since in order to see or hear ghosts, it is necessary either to have been barn with the faculty, and, consequently, literally live in bath worlds at once, or, that some person be present, from whose body vital magnetism escapes in sufficient quantities to render the contact of the inhabitants of the two worlds possible, who shall say that this necessary vital magnetism does not escape from the bodies of the insane, as well as those of the sane, or, that those sane persons born with the faculty of seeing and hearing ghosts, or who have became possessed of it, and are hence in an abnormal state - must lose it when they have become insane. Many insane persons are undoubtedly "possessed of devils" or, in more modern phraseology, are entirely under the malign influence of evil ghosts whom they can at times both see and hear.

If we class among the deranged all the persons who today see and hear ghosts, as the medical fraternity would have us do, simply because we know that those among the insane often claim to see and hear ghosts - what is to be thought of all those supermundane portions of the Bible, the Koran, the Talmud, the sacred books of India, and the ancient writings of the Chinese. Were the accounts of ghosts, angels and devils, that are to be found in each and all of them, written by insane men, or did the writers tell the truth in narrating the actual experiences of sane men? Notwithstanding the unanimous verdict of materialistic physicians, some persons who have been pronounced sane, or who are at least accredited with being of sound mind, believe the latter; and that so far as those ancient writers could convey accounts of what they saw and heard of good and evil ghosts, they chronicled the truth.

As the term "astral body" may be obscure to some readers, I must explain that by it I mean what all Christian teachers call the soul, and that, by the term "vital magnetism," I mean that subtle principle that should probably be more correctly called human electricity - that permeates, and holds the astral body to the physical body, or, as we may say, the soul to its earthly form, from which it is released by death, at which change the vital magnetism accompanies the soul to where the soul, or astral body, as I prefer to call it, exists forever - the world of ghosts.

In reference to the well-known and easily corroborated fact that persons who have lost limbs, or portions thereof, feel at times that they are again actually present, I would say that, although imagination may, in one case in a hundred, account for the phenomenon, the medical theory about memory, and the ends of the irritated nerves in the remaining portion of the limb, is, nevertheless, a mistake, although it is possible that the fact of the ends of the nerves in the stump of the severed member being inflamed may, in some instances, occasionally cause the elimination of sufficient vital magnetism from the physical and astral bodies of the sufferer to allow the presence of the astral or ghostly portion of the limb to be again felt, as if present in its earthly or physical form. However, as the ghostly or astral limb is still present, and, under certain other vital magnetic conditions, its actual presence is often manifested when there is no irritation, it must be obvious that it is not necessary that irritation of the ends of the severed nerves should always be present when the presence of the amputated limb is apparent.

This article is not the proper place for me to give a detailed account of my weirdly wonderful experience with the six ghosts of the dead, in the haunted house where I had an opportunity, such as befalls but few men on the earth, to study the supermundane.

All that I need say is that I kept a journal of all that occurred concerning the great Amherst mystery, and can assure my readers that I was not deceived by jugglers, charlatans, or the alleged mediums of Modern Spiritualism, for no such persons were at any time living in, or visiting the house during the time I lived there, nor at any previous or subsequent time, and I may add that I am not, and never have been, a hypnotic subject, nor capable of being influenced, in any way whatsoever, by psychology in any of its other forms - not even the psychology of Modern Spiritualism.

For 17 years I have been a careful and patient investigator of the supermundane, and, during that period, have had ample opportunity to expose fraud, and to corroborate what I found to be the truth concerning the greatest problem of human life.

"Is there another world and a life hereafter?" is a question asked today by millions of the human race. I answer, most emphatically, "Yes, and the fact is capable of scientific demonstration, and need no longer rest on faith and belief."

In closing, I must say that I have found during my investigations, that just as surely as vital magnetism escapes from the persons of individuals in quantities sufficient to render possible contact between them and ghosts, just as surely does the same kind of vital magnetism escape from some ghosts; and that that is why such ghosts, without the aid of the vital magnetism escaping from the body of a person in the physical form, can, and do come amongst mankind on earth, frequently haunting old houses that have been deserted by men, and, in all probability, occasionally committing terrible crimes that are charged to men, and for which innocent men have undoubtedly been made to suffer.

It is a fallacy to believe that ghosts are ever ethereal, because they appear so to the eyes of men; on the contrary, they are always, in reality, just as substantial beings as we are, and can come in contact with our world and us, with great ease when compared to the difficulty we often experience in coming in contact with them.

All men appear to be semi-transparent when they are seen by ghosts, for, as I have already stated, the fact is proved by my investigations what is a solid substance to us as men, is to the ghosts but a liquid or vapor, while what to them is solid substance, is to us but air.

There is not the slightest doubt in my mind, nor can there be in the mind of any man, or body of scientific men, living in a haunted house, that the evil ghosts of evil men still haunt mankind, as they did in the days of Jesus and His disciples. But the ghosts of the good, the ghosts of the pure in heart-ah! how sad it is to have to record that my experience has convinced me that the ghosts of the good and pure rarely come to visit the friends and loved ones whom they have left behind, and I believe the reason is that the corruption, the evil among the people of the earth is so predominant, in the majority of instances, that, being unable to benefit us by their return, they consequently make no effort to rend for all time the veil that separates the world of the good and pure ghosts from the world of depraved mankind.

REPORT OF A PERSONAL INVESTIGATION INTO "THE GREAT AMHERST MYSTERY" BY HEREWARD CARRINGTON

From the book, *Personal Experiences in Spiritualism*

An American paranormal researcher, Hereward Carrington, investigated the Amherst case in 1907, interviewing surviving witnesses. His independent findings have been included here to support the testimony of Walter Hubbell.

In January, 1907, I traveled to Windsor, Nova Scotia, in order to investigate the case of "poltergeist " that had been reported to the Society for Psychical Research. These accounts had been coming in for some time, and it seemed probable that genuine phenomena had been observed. The result of my investigation of that case, however, was to show that nothing but trickery had been involved throughout, and that fraud was the sufficient explanation of the whole case from start to finish. As I had to go back to New York through Amherst, and as my interest in that case had been already aroused by a reading of Mr. Hubbell's book, I decided to "stop off " at Amherst and gather what first-hand information I could on the actual scene of operations. Accordingly, I spent the best part of two days (January 26-27, 1907) in interviewing what witnesses I could find (who were still alive) and in visiting the house in question.

The great majority of the witnesses unfortunately proved to be dead - Parson Townsend, Mr. Robb, Doctor Nathan Tupper, Doctor Carritte, and others who might have proved excellent witnesses had they been still alive, all had passed into the Great Beyond, and with them their testimony for or against "The Great Amherst Mystery." Nor could I find any trace of Jennie Cox, the elder sister, who witnessed the greater part of the phenomena, nor John Teed nor William Cox. All had died or moved from Amherst. Mr. and Mrs. Teed, however, are still alive, and the latter gave me a great deal of valuable information, which I give herewith, Mr. Hubbell has collected the testimony of some 16 more witnesses of the phenomena - still living - which greatly strengthens the evidential value of the case. In spite of the fact that my interview with the "medium" herself (Esther Cox) did not prove as satisfactory as it might have been, the case is, however, far stronger than when Mr. Hubbell first published his book more than 20 years ago.

It is fortunate that this investigation, tardy as it is, has been made before all the first-hand witnesses - including the medium herself - have died, and all chance of personal investigation lost forever.

The following is a copy, almost verbatim, of my original series of notes, made immediately upon my return to the hotel after interviewing the Teed family in Amherst in 1907.

"I called on the Teeds today. They have moved from their old house, which is now occupied by a Mrs. Cahill She knew of the phenomena, and appeared to believe in them; but stated that nothing of the sort had appeared since her occupancy of the house. Since the Teeds had left the house, it had been entirely renovated, re-papered, etc., so that all the markings on the walls, the burnt timbers, and so forth, were entirely covered up. Unfortunately, therefore, these can no longer be seen. The house is a small, single house, quite detached from those on either side of it by some 12 feet, and presents the appearance of isolation and desolation. It is so small that one cannot conceive how any person could be concealed within it without instant detection, while it is certain that no one could have remained long upon the low roof without discovery."

"Having taken a good look at the house, inside and out, I called upon the Teeds, whose new address I had ascertained from Mrs. Cahill. Mrs. Teed struck me as a quick, active woman, alert and quick in thought and action. She appeared to be a very good witness. She remembered very well all that had transpired, and agreed that Mr. Hubbell had accurately outlined the phenomena in his book, though she added that she thought he had dramatized and embellished it in places. Mrs. Teed said that she had a copy of the book which she had read through, but had not looked at it for years. Her manner appeared to me perfectly natural, and I was struck at the time by her absence of desire to make capital out of the affair. If she had wished to bring a certain degree of notoriety upon herself and family, she would have elaborated and gloated over the incidents; but such was by no means the case. She took a natural interest in it, but that was all. Her manner certainly impressed me very favorably.

"I asked her if any fraud had ever been discovered in connection with the case. Mrs. Teed assured me that, so far as she knew, nothing of the sort had been discovered at the time, and none had ever come to light since. Her own faith in the reality of the facts had obviously remained unshaken. She gave me Esther Cox's address in Massachusetts, and talked freely with me about the whole case. I asked her opinion of several of the phenomena, but in nearly every case her memory was clear and her testimony confirmatory. She told me that the independent voices in the air, the writing on the wall, were all terrible realities, and that no explanation of these facts had ever been found. The whole family had been terrified, and had searched constantly for the causes of these phenomena, but always unsuccessfully. I asked particularly concerning the incident in which a bucket of cold water had bubbled and apparently boiled on the table while she was looking at it, and without apparent cause. She remembered this clearly, and assured me that it was 'an exact fact,' as described. She added that the water frothed at the same time, but stated that it remained cool. She saw this several times. Esther Cox was standing close by the pail on every occasion, but Mrs. Teed assured me that Esther did not touch the pail, and that her (Esther's) hands were visible to her throughout. The first time this occurred, she observed Esther through a crack in the door, thinking that she might be playing some trick, but saw that she did not approach the pail on the table, the water in which, nevertheless, acted as she had described.

"At first, I was told, phenomena would happen when Esther was ill in bed, and when she certainly could not have produced the phenomena herself, even had she wished to. Knocks were heard, and great patches of the plastering came down with the force of the blows. Sometimes, however, the plaster would come down in exact squares as though cut cleanly through with a knife. The pillows were often snatched away from under Esther's head, while other members of the family were looking on; and the pillows would be blown up like a balloon, to the bursting point. The sheets were also snatched away - just as Mr. Hubbell has said in his book - and would stand on end in the center of the room. As soon as anyone attempted to grab these sheets, however, they would collapse and fall to the floor. Mrs. Teed added that it was certainly very 'funny.' All this was common property at the time, it appeared, and many people came to observe the phenomena. At times, as many as a hundred people would be present at once, looking on, as the various events transpired.

"When the family had grown accustomed to the happenings, they would sometimes be amused at them, and then Esther would laugh too. She seemed to observe the facts from an outside point of view, just as did the rest of the family. It was true, Mrs. Teed informed me, that Esther Cox had been cut and had been stuck with pins, just as Mr. Hubbell narrated; and she added that this would often happen at meal times, when Esther was engaged in eating, and when both her hands were visible. On such occasions pins had often been stuck into her very deeply. On being questioned, however, Mrs. Teed admitted that she had never seen an object start on its journey through the air, and, so far as she could remember, she had never actually seen it in the air. It had invariably finished its journey when she observed it. (This rang true, and in my estimation went a long way toward proving her perfect honesty in the narrative she was giving me. For example, the cover of the sugar bowl was found missing. A slight noise would be heard, and the cover had disappeared! Two hours later this cover was found behind Esther on the sofa upon which she had been sitting. On the contrary, Mrs. Teed had seen the lid of a trunk open and close several times apparently of its own accord, when she was looking at it, and when Esther was seen to be in another part of the room.)

"Mrs. Teed then told me of one or two incidents of interest that had occurred, and which she clearly remembered, but which are not in Mr. Hubbell's book. One such incident is the following: Mrs. Teed and Esther Cox were washing the dishes together in the kitchen, no one else being present. Mrs. Teed was engaged in washing the dishes, and Esther in drying them. The dishpan, containing a handful of silver, was half full of water, when Esther turned and walked to the stove at the opposite end of the kitchen, to get some more hot water. Her back was turned to the dishpan, and she was about three feet away from it when suddenly it jumped into the air, turned completely over, and fell to the floor with a crash, spilling the water and the silver all over the floor! Mrs. Teed was sure that, on that occasion, Esther was not near the pan, and that she could not have touched it.

"Another such incident is the following: On one occasion Esther was asleep in one room, Mr. and Mrs. Teed being in the room across the hall, and both doors being open.

"Esther was asleep in bed. Mr. and Mrs. Teed's bed was in the room on the opposite side of the hall, and from it they could see Esther, in the opposite room across the hall, through the doors, both of which were open. At the end of the hall were the stairs; first a flight of three, then a straight flight, leading down to the ground floor. Under these conditions, and while Esther was asleep in her bed (so Mrs. Teed assured me) articles of furniture - chiefly chairs - were taken out of Esther's room and thrown downstairs, a distance of 15 or 20 feet. They could be seen to come out of the door of Esther's room, pass noisily along the floor of the hall to the top of the stairs, tumble down the flight of three steps, turn the corner and tumble down the remaining flight of steps to the floor below. All this while Esther was motionless in bed!

"I was also told other items of interest. Doctor Carritte, it was said, would frequently place his hat on the bed while examining Esther, and it would be thrown to the floor violently. All could see that Esther had not touched it, or moved in any way. On one occasion, the baby was taken out of the cot, and deposited very gently upon the floor. Loud knocks were heard in all parts of the house, and particularly in the cellar; but investigation always proved fruitless. On one occasion, Esther was tied to her chair and carefully watched, but still the thumps and bangs continued on the walls, floor, and in the cellar of the house. While these demonstrations were going on, some of the family went into the cellar to investigate, but could find nothing to account for the noise, which, nevertheless, continued on the floor directly over their heads! Esther's presence seemed necessary to ensure phenomena, however, and in her absence nothing happened.

"I asked Mrs. Teed if she remembered the remarkable bodily swellings from which Esther suffered at the time. She replied that she did, and that Mr. Hubbell's account was quite accurate in this respect. The trouble was caused in this manner. Esther had been told to place glass in her shoes 'to prevent the escape of electricity from her body!' and the result was that she had swollen up in the manner indicated. As soon as the glass had been removed from her shoes, the swelling subsided, and she felt immediate relief!

"On another occasion, Mrs. Teed told me, she had seen a number of chairs piled one on the top of another, before her eyes, until a pile of five or six had been made, and then the bottom chair suddenly withdrawn, and the whole pile tumble to the floor. Frequently, furniture had been shaken and knocked about in this manner until it was 'all nicked and dented.' I examined the chairs - the identical ones which had been used by the intelligences for this famous 'juggling feat'; and, sure enough, they were badly dented, and showed unmistakable evidences of having been roughly handled and thrown about. I also examined the paperweight which Mr. Hubbell mentioned, and found it solid, heavy and badly nicked in one corner. It could certainly have done considerable damage had it been thrown with force.

"Esther herself had been greatly afraid, especially at first, and would never stay in a room alone, if she could help it. Her bed would be shaken, when she retired for the night, until she was worn out from fear and lack of sleep. Everyone wished that the phenomena would cease, but they continued, in spite of all their efforts to prevent them. No fraud was discovered at any time, however, then or later, and Mrs. Teed was sure that none had been practiced at the time.

"It may be objected to all this, of course, that I give the confirmatory evidence of only one person, and that person the sister of 'the medium,' one who would naturally wish to shield her younger sister against all charges of fraud or imposture.

As to the first point, that is, fortunately, answered by the additional evidence which Mr. Hubbell has been enabled to gather. As to the latter objection, I can only say that I think Mrs. Teed too fair-minded to protect her sister from public criticism if she had found her, either at the time, or subsequently, to have been guilty of fraud. Evident precautions were taken at the time to prevent this, and, as I have said before, the whole household (not to speak of outsiders) were on the constant look-out to prevent it. Further, it Mrs. Teed had felt that she should protect her sister at the time, I do not think that she would feel bound to do so now, after a lapse of nearly 30 years, when all the novelty and notoriety has worn off, and all the 'glory' - such as it was - might have been supposed to have been achieved years ago!

Esther Cox is now married, and living in another part of the world altogether; she has not seen her sister, Mrs. Olive Teed, for a number of years. Must we suppose that, in spite of this, the whole family, and not only they, but all the other witnesses in the case, would persist in sticking to a lie, simply to defend the absent Esther Cox? It is incredible! Whatever the interpretation of the facts, I am quite sure that Esther alone was responsible for them; and that all the other members of the family are entirely innocent of any participation therein."

So much, then, I concluded from my investigation at Amherst. The principal witness, however, had yet to be interviewed, viz. Esther Cox herself; and she I proposed to interview as soon as I reached Boston.

On arriving in Boston, then, on my way back to New York, I went to see Esther Cox and found her living in a small cottage. She stated, very reluctantly, in reply to my questions, that the "power" had not visited her since her marriage, but gave the distinct impression that she still believed in the phenomena. Pressed with questions, she stated that she would not talk about the case, as she was "afraid they would come back." She showed great reluctance to discuss the story at all. She appeared to be angry with her sister, Mrs. Teed, for having given me her address, and with Mr. Hubbell for having written the book; not that she did not still believe in the phenomena, apparently, or was in any way inclined to admit fraud on her own part, but she did not wish to discuss it at all, and appeared simply irritated whenever it was mentioned. The more I pressed her with questions, the more irritated she became, and finally her husband intervened, and said that for $100 he would consent to her telling me all necessary details, but not unless! I said to him frankly that I should, in that case, have no guarantee whatever that I was not furnished with a hundred dollars' worth of lies - as bought testimony - particularly in a case of this character - would be absolutely worthless. It being useless waste of time to prolong the interview, I put on my hat and left, none too pleased with the interview, or the late medium and her husband.

After returning to New York it struck me that I might have received a wrong impression of Esther Cox herself, simply because of her husband's attitude; so I wrote to my friend, Mr. Herbert B. Turner, then living in Boston, and asked him to look up her record, if possible, and let me know the result. He was not enabled to do so himself, but asked the wife of a very old friend of his to investigate for him, and report her findings. I give her letter below. Concerning Mrs. H - - , the lady who undertook the investigation, Mr. Turner writes:

"Gray H., the husband of Grace H., is a lifelong friend of mine. We grew up as brothers, and I know he would not draw upon his imagination.

Grace H I do not know except as a speaking acquaintance, as she was a Brockton girl and he an Arlington fellow. However, she looks to be a matter-of-fact and sensible woman, and I have been told that she impresses all who know her as a girl of sterling qualities..."

The following is Mrs. H's report:

"My Dear Mr. Turner,

As I am considerably more familiar with Brockton and its people than Gray is, he turned your letter over to me for investigation, and I can now report as follows:

"From a department of this city I have learned that Esther Cox is a very hard-working woman, respectable, honest, and reliable. In fact, the department officials consider her as one of their very best workers. They tell me that during the four years she has been known to them they have found her square in all her dealings with them, and perfectly truthful - this last having been verified at various times, when they had investigated statements made by her, and found them always true; and they say they would not hesitate to take her word as to this old experience of hers, as she is not at all of an imaginative turn of mind, and would not be likely to make up any such thing.

"In regard to that experience, however, she could not be induced to say a word; said it was something she 'dared not talk about.' It is quite possible that fear of her husband keeps her silent. Whatever the reason, no satisfaction could be got from her answers to this question, and so they gave up trying.

"I am sorry we could find out so little for you, but hope even this little bit of information may be of some assistance to you.

"Sincerely,

"Grace R. H.

"4th February, 1907"

It will be observed that this agrees with my own experience almost exactly. I could not induce Esther Cox to make any statement to me, apparently for the same reason: she was "afraid of their coming back." Late testimony as to her character and veracity has, therefore, been favorable, rather than the reverse; and her honesty and sincerity have been largely vindicated. To this extent, therefore, the "poltergeist" phenomena in "The Great Amherst Mystery" have received additional confirmation and support.

APPENDIX II
FROM OLD NEWSPAPERS

ESTHER COX
[From the *Amherst Gazette*, June 27, 1879]

The manifestations in presence of this young lady have recently been of a very lively character. She is now staying at Mr. Teed's.

The case has lately been watched closely by Mr. Walter Hubbell, who has seen similar phenomena, and has determined to spend some time in its investigation. He has frequently caught bogus "mediums" in their deceptions, and considers that Miss Cox could not easily deceive him if she were inclined to do so. He informs us that he has heard knocks, at times very loud, and that these have denoted the dates on coins in his pocket, time of day, etc.; that on different days the heavy cover of a stone-china sugar bowl disappeared from the breakfast table, and afterwards dropped from the air in the room; that when he asked for matches for lighting his pipe they dropped in front of him on several occasions; that chairs, tables, and a lounge were upset, and various articles were thrown from 10 to 30 feet.

THE AMHERST MYSTERY
[From the *Western Chronicle*, Kentville, Nova Scotia, Wednesday, July 16, 1879]

The *Amherst Gazette* publishes about two columns of a journal kept by Walter Hubbell, while boarding at Daniel Teed's to investigate the "Amherst Mystery." The narrative records the observations made by Mr. Hubbell, and contains some very remarkable, not to say tough statements. These, for instance: "June 25th, I have been pulling pins out of Esther, all day, which the invisible power has been sticking into all parts of her person. I have seen the pins come out of the air and stick into the girl; they have also been put into her ears. I pulled about 30 pins out of her today. It is becoming more wonderful and unaccountable. A chair was taken out of my bedroom and thrown down stairs after Esther Cox, no person being in the upper part of the house at the time. As we were entering the parlor this afternoon, both saw a chair fall over and jump up again, and were both five feet from it at the time."

The vagaries of household furniture, in Esther's presence, are certainly astonishing, according to Mr. Hubbell's description, and must render the Teed domicile anything but a quiet boarding house, while the habit that carving knives, paperweights, and other articles appear to have of flying at boarders, must be more exciting than agreeable. It is certainly surprising, with all the boasted scientific discoveries of the nineteenth century, that no solution of these mysterious manifestations can be found, and that nothing can be done to prevent their recurrence.

[From *The Banner of Light*, Boston, Saturday, July 12, 1879]

We have cited on several occasions the case of Miss Esther Cox, the singular phenomena occurring in whose presence have created so much interest and popular excitement in Nova Scotia. The subject has arisen once more (after a temporary subsidence) on the wave of discussion, and we have before us in the way of proof thereof a copy of the *Amherst Gazette*, for June 27th, and a letter from Walter Hubbell, dated the 25th of last month, both of which set the matter forth in plain language. The *Gazette* says:

"The manifestations in the presence of this young lady (Esther Cox) have recently been of a very lively character. She is now staying at Mr. Teed's.
The case has lately been watched closely by Mr. Walter Hubbell, who has determined to spend some time in its investigation."

APPENDIX III
LETTERS AND SWORN
STATEMENTS

DR. CARRITTE TO PROFESSOR PEASE

Dr. Thomas W. Carritte, was born in Amherst, Nova Scotia, March 23, 1830, and died in Abington, Va., November 9, 1885.

AMHERST, NOVA SCOTIA,
February 3, 1883

Dear, Sir:

In reply to your letter of inquiry I take this occasion to say that my long silence has been due not to carelessness or inattention, but to necessity. I should have written you much earlier but for a severe injury to the knee joint with which I have been confined to bed. I take my pen in hand at this comparatively late moment to say that what Mr. Walter Hubbell has published about the mysterious Esther Cox case is entirely correct, as doctors not only, but clergymen, editors and perhaps hundreds of other persons from their own independent observations could testify. The young lady was a patient of mine previous to and during those wonderful demonstrations and, with all the rest, I must acknowledge that I was sorely puzzled. I tried various experiments, but with no satisfactory results. I even had her placed on a thoroughly insulated bed, in the center of the room, with reference to possible electric currents, but in vain.

Honestly skeptical persons were on all occasions soon convinced that there was no fraud or deception in the case. It would take me an entire week to write you a full history of my connection with those strange doings. Were I to publish the case in the medical journals, I doubt if it would be believed by physicians generally - I am certain I could not have believed such apparent miracles had I not witnessed them. I have preserved all of the press correspondence on the subject and could bring, if necessary, at least 50 people of prominence and character to substantiate all, and indeed very much more than Mr. Hubbell has set forth.

T. W. CARRITTE

STATE OF PENNSYLVANIA, City and County of Philadelphia

Prof. Rufus D. Pease, being duly sworn, deposes and says that this letter is a true copy of the letter he received from Doctor T. W. Carritte, of Amherst, Nova Scotia, dated February third, eighteen hundred and eighty three.

Affirmed and subscribed to before me this 28th day of June, 1889.

J. R. MASSEY, Notary Public

Letter from the late Arthur Davison, Esq., Clerk of County Court, Amherst, Nova Scotia, to F. E. Morgan.

[Copied from *The Central Ray Magazine*, Vol. 17, May, 1893.]

Amherst, Nova Scotia, April 24, 1893

FRED E. MORGAN,

Your letter of the 19th, inst. Addressed to the Superintendent of the High School, Amherst (E. J. Lay), has been handed to me. Mr. Lay did not live at Amherst at the time and has asked me to reply for him.

I do not believe in Spiritualism. My own idea is that in some way the magnetic power in this girl became unhinged. I hope that your study and research may unfold this to the world. Esther Cox worked for me for three months and a better one we never had since we have been married, (20 years). I have often watched her to find out how she came down stairs, she seemed to fly. It proved a bad day for me before she left, as she burned my barn. I may say in passing I read the book published by Hubbell, and while he painted the facts up to make the book sell, the facts were there all the same. She was not good looking, very ignorant, only a common education, could read and write but not spell. She was very much afraid of it. I tried several times to teach her to exert control of her will power, but just as I had gained a point she became afraid and would go no further nor do anything. My house and where she lived before she came to live with me was about 50 yards distant and I used to call often to see how she got along. Hundreds did the same.

At first it was only rapping and pounding, but at times it assumed a more serious aspect. One night as I was on my way home, I met the Doctor who attended her (Dr. Carritte since dead). He asked me to go with him and see Esther, as he feared she was going to die. He had then tried everything to arouse her from a semi-unconscious state and as a last resort was going to try a battery. When I saw her, she was on a cot bed, and seemed to be dead, but for a violent heaving of her body that is from her breast down to her legs, she would fill up and lift the clothes as you inflate a bladder and then it would suddenly collapse. Those spells came in regular order, about every minute. While the doctor was getting ready, I watched her in company with her sister and husband, expecting her death every moment, but all at once we heard tappings on the foot board, at first faint and then louder and louder, when all at once she opened her eyes and in a few moments spoke to us, and soon rallied, was up on the next day, but weak. She had several of these turns but this one I saw; but it is hard to describe it fully but it was the hardest scene I ever witnessed.

Another: One evening while living with me she was putting the things on the table for tea (I had told her not to leave the drawer where the forks were kept open but this time she forgot). I was reading the paper not paying any attention to her, but I happened at the time to be sitting between her and the drawer. The first thing I knew a dinner fork struck me on the back of the head. Some people may doubt these things but when a man gets a whack on the head it then with him at least, assumes a reality.

Another: And this was the only thing that gave me any fright; I kept a horse and a cow at the time. Esther used to milk the cow. I attended the horse myself. The cow stood at the further end of the barn (say 25 feet from the door) where I kept a box with my curry comb and brushes. This particular evening she had just finished milking and met me at the door. As I stepped inside I saw my curry comb running along the floor about eight or ten feet behind her. You may depend that I stepped out of the way quick too. It struck the door post. I then picked it up, and after that I kept the key in my pocket. The next evening when I came home she wanted the key to go and milk. I handed it to her, she had the milk bucket in her other hand, and just as our hands met, a large two-quart dipper of water, which had been on the table struck our hands and spilled the water over the both of us, giving me a pretty good wetting, spoiling my cuffs. It appears she had just been using this dipper but it was sitting six or eight feet from us and had to pass through an open door at right angles to get where it did.

My wife saw ashes, tea leaves, scrubbing brushes, soap and mop rags and an old ham bone often flying around and sometimes it put them out in their work, but we got so used to it we put up with all these things as it was hard at the time to get help; especially help like her, until she set my barn on fire, we then had her put in jail, since then I don't know if she has had any of her turns. She got married, married poor, and has several children. I can't give her name, but if it is of any use to you I will give it.

What I have written may not be what you want, as you know in writing such things offhand they are not half done. Please let me hear from you, and if I can say anything more will be happy to do so.

ARTHUR DAVISON,
Clerk of County Court

NOTE: All the fires started in Daniel Teed's home were set by the demon-ghost, Bob. I know this fact to be indisputable and there can be no doubt whatsoever that this same fire fiend burned Davison's barn. - WALTER HUBBELL

FROM DR. RICHARD HODGSON

The following letter from the late Dr. Hodgson was in reply to a letter from me asking for copies of any further data In his possession concerning the "Amherst Mystery" so that I could use it in future additions to my book on the case. I knew Hodgson for 17 years and knew him well. I have many letters from him and the one here given dated "July 20, 1905," is the last I ever received from this great investigator and champion of the truth. During our last conversation in his office in Boston on April 17, 1903, he gave me a copy of the Proceedings of the Society for Psychical Research Part XXXIII, Vol. XIII, February, 1898 *containing a review by Andrew Lang, of one of Podmore's books. In this review Lang alludes to the "Amherst Mystery". The book of "Dreams and Ghosts" by Andrew Lang in which this distinguished writer quotes profusely from my work is also reviewed in the same copy of the Proceedings. Mr. Lang wrote me from Highhead Castle, Carlisle, Scotland, in June, 1905, that, "he had no fresh information as to the Amherst affair." He had not only read my first edition of this book (1888) but also the letter from Arthur Davison, of Amherst, written to F. E. Morgan in 1893, and now given in this edition of my work.*

"AMERICAN BRANCH OF THE SOCIETY FOR PSYCHICAL RESEARCH."
Richard Hodgson, L.L.D.,
Secretary and Treasurer
BOSTON, MASS.
July 20th, 1905.

DEAR MR. HUBBELL:

In reply to yours of July 6th, we have looked through our files of documents but are unable to find any report made by Professor James, on the "Amherst Mystery" case. My own recollection is that Professor James was unable to visit Nova Scotia himself, but got a student of his to make inquiries there, and that this student sent a report to him, but that no additional evidence of any special importance was forthcoming, owing doubtless to the lapse of time since the events and owing, I fancy, partly to the lack of personal interest in the enquiry on the part of the student.

I am giving you just my own personal recollection. I have written to Professor James to tell him that I cannot find any memoranda by him in our files and to ask him if he can lay his hands on the report of the student. It is probable that he sent me the report at the time and that I may have sent it to England. I sent various important cases with the results of the inquiries to England many years ago which, owing to neglect over there, got entombed.

I believe, however, that I am right in saying that in any case such enquiries as were made later on, did not contribute anything that would be of importance for you to add to any future edition of your book.

If we can lay our hands upon any memoranda in connection with the case I shall be glad to send them to you.

Yours sincerely,

R. HODGSON

I have compared the foregoing letter with the original and hereby certify that this is a correct copy.

ELIZABETH CATHERINE HUBBELL.
June 29th, 1908
Brooklyn, New York

LETTER FROM PROFESSOR JAMES

SILVER LAKE, N. H.
June 20, 1909

DEAR MR. HUBBELL:

George H. Kent, bookseller, Cambridge, has the Joan of Arc tickets for sale. I heard some time ago that all were sold, however, and I fear that in any event this will reach you too late.

I shall write to Froggatt for a copy of your new edition. It has been a tremendous pity that no evidence extraneous to your account has ever been got on that extraordinary case.

Sincerely yours,

WM. JAMES*

Prof. James, never having read this new edition, was not aware of the valuable corroborative evidence it contains and doubtless would have been highly gratified by the testimony I have fortunately secured after the lapse of 30 years.

WALTER HUBBELL

LETTER FROM MRS. DANIEL TEED, SISTER OF ESTHER COX

AMHERST, Nova Scotia
June 21, 1908

WALTER HUBBELL, Amherst, Nova Scotia

Dear Friend:

Mr. Teed and myself have read your book on Esther and the ghosts or demons and there is one thing you have not got that should be in the book.

On Sunday night after we were all in bed, Esther being in her own room, having come in from Van Amburgh's to stay with us over night before going to live at Arthur Davison's after you had gone away from Amherst, and Jane being away for that night, the following occurred:

It was about ten o'clock, Esther was in her bed, and as you know her room was opposite mine and Mr. Teed's. Our doors were both open and we could both look into her room, for it was moonlight. We saw a chair slide across her room from the wall, and when it was near her bed, close up to it, the pillow under her head came out and settled down on the chair. Esther could see Maggie Fisher, the ghost, dressed all in white, sit down on the pillow on the chair, but we could not see her at all. Maggie then rubbed Esther from head to foot under the bedclothes and then began to pinch her on the arms and neck and then to scratch her body with a hair-pin we found in the bed next day. Esther said she could not stand it any longer. Bob, the ghost, then got to work and threw all the furniture except the bedstead out of the room into the entry. Esther could see him do it, we could only see things come out and see that she lay there in the bed still and quiet.

After the furniture had been all thrown out of the room, Bob commenced to rock and shake the bed as Esther lay there in it. The noise was so great we could not sleep, so Mr. Teed, at my request, went into her room and took Esther's mattress off her bed and brought it into our room, where he put it on the floor at the foot of our bed so we could all go to sleep for, as you know, Bob and Maggie, the ghosts, did not like Daniel (Mr. Teed) any more than they did you, although they never tried to kill him as Bob did you with the glass paper weight you remember, which I still have after all these years.

All the demons could work better in our cottage on Princess Street than anywhere else, and they were afraid to do much in our room when

Mr. Teed was in it because they did not want him to say Esther must go away for fear all would be burned up by Bob, as we nearly were. Well, after the mattress had been brought into our room and Esther was lying on it, the ghosts took hold of the lid of an old trunk in our room that was not locked, but shut down, and gave it just one parting slam as a good night; nothing else occurred and we all went to sleep in peace.

I still have the lounge on which you lay when Bob threw the glass paperweight at your head, also six of the chairs that they used to pile up and throw over and around in our parlor. You may put all this in the new edition of your book if you choose. Daniel has no objection, for it is all true, like the rest you have.

OLIVE TEED

STATE OF NEW YORK, City and County of New York

WALTER HUBBELL, being duly sworn, deposes, and says: That the letters; essay on "The Supermundane," the chapter headed "Thirty Years After," "Document from Citizen of Amherst," and all other reading matter in this edition of his book "The Great Amherst Mystery," were respectively written to him, written by him, or sent to him for publication; and that the same are true copies as placed in the printer's hands; for this edition only.

WALTER HUBBELL.

Sworn to before me this 9th day of February, 1916.
WM. BRADFORD,
Notary Public, Kings County,
Certificate filed in N. Y. County,
(No. 69)

NOTARY'S CERTIFICATE

NEW YORK, February 9, 1916.
This is to certify that Walter Hubbell is hereby authorized to print my notary seal on the affidavit he has sworn to before me for the purpose of attaching same to his book, entitled "The Great Amherst Mystery."

WM. BRADFORD, Notary Public, Kings County,
Certificate Filed in N. Y. Co.
No. 69.
476 Fifth Avenue, New York City

TESTAMENTARY DOCUMENT

Presented to Walter Hubbell, by citizens of Amherst, Nova Scotia, in June, 1908 - 29 years after he had lived in the haunted home of Esther Cox.

We, the undersigned inhabitants of the Town of Amherst, County of Cumberland, Province of Nova Scotia, and Dominion of Canada in British America:

Having of our own personal knowledge and not by or through hearsay or belief, absolutely known, seen and heard individually all or some of the demonstrations, manifestations, and communications of an invisible, intelligent and malicious power within the atmosphere that continued its awe-inspiring and mysterious operations in the home of Daniel Teed, 6 Princess Street, Amherst, Nova Scotia, and elsewhere in the actual presence of his sister-in-law, Esther Cox (but never manifested itself during her absence from the house), and continued to manifest itself for the period of one year from 1878 to 1879, as narrated by Walter Hubbell the actor (who lived a boarder in the aforesaid house) in a book written by him entitled "The Great Amherst Mystery. A True Narrative of the Supernatural," which account having been read by us and being known to us as accurate and truthful as to all and each fact, particulars and description given in the aforesaid book, we hereto, of our own free will, affix our names to this testamentary paper so that it may be printed in all future editions of the aforesaid book and go before the world in corroboration and verification of what actually transpired in the presence of the Teed family, Walter Hubbell, and hundreds of the inhabitants of Amherst, including ourselves, some 30 ago.

Signed by us and delivered to Walter Hubbell whom we each know personally, this tenth day of June A. D., 1908.

(Signed)

Daniel Teed	William Ripley
Olive Teed	David T. Chapman
Neander Quigley	John W. Stewart
J. A. Simpson	Lawrence White
Arthur W. Moffatt	Rufus Hicks
J. Albert Black	Charles Tupper Hillson
Silas A. McNutt	Ephraim T. Chapman
William Beattie	Barry D. Bent

CPSIA information can be obtained at www.ICGtesting.com
Printed in the USA
LVOW13s1856080814

398214LV00021B/956/P